Introducing
Computer Security

Michael B Wood FBCS

PUBLISHED BY NCC PUBLICATIONS

British Library Cataloguing in Publication Data

Wood, Michael B., FBCS
    Introducing computer security
    1. Electronic data processing department –
    Security measures
    I. Title
    658.4'78   HF5548.2

ISBN 0-85012-340-2

For Rosemary   7300 2

First published in 1982 by:

NCC Publications, The National Computing Centre Limited, Oxford Road, Manchester, M1 7ED, England.

Typeset in 11 pt Times Roman and printed by UPS Blackburn Limited, 76-80 Northgate, Blackburn, Lancashire.

ISBN 0-85012-340-2

Preface

Computer security is of growing concern throughout data processing for business and administration. Systems are more complex and are under changing threats, both accidental and deliberate.

Introducing Computer Security is for all those using and managing data processing systems. It aims to create a greater understanding and awareness of the current problems and some of the solutions. The Centre has been active in computer security for ten years. The book draws heavily upon that work, and I am grateful for the help of many friends and colleagues, especially Tony Squires, Les Waring and John Pritchard. Geoff Simons was most helpful as Editor. All of us in computer security owe much to that pioneer, the late Ray Ellison.

Contents

1 Introduction

Computer security is a a vast subject. It ranges over physical security of buildings, fire protection, software and hardware, personnel policies and financial audit and control. Data security and confidentiality of personal data is regulated by law in several countries, giving rise to further concern. There are legal problems about computer fraud and other kinds of misuse. Clearly therefore this book can only give a broad insight into the subject. It makes no attempt to give a complete picture. Rather, the aim is to create an understanding of the general principles of security, especially as they apply to computer systems in business and administration.

Some appreciation of computers and their use in data processing is assumed. The expert might perhaps quarrel with some of my simplifications. I have deliberately avoided technical details, which change very rapidly here, as elsewhere in information technology.

There is a very real gap in current awareness and understanding: computer security is a corporate need. Data processing of itself does not need security – it is the organisation that needs it. All evidence shows that a satisfactory security programme needs support from all parts of an organisation. The threats are increasing, as is the dependence of organisations upon computers. Everyone in business and administration – most of us in fact – needs computer security.

The next chapter gives an overview of security principles. The following chapters (3-8) discuss various aspects of security, to give a feel for the subject. Chapter 9 covers risk management, including risk analysis and control. This is now a specialised art, and there are in fact several firms who do nothing else. Contingency planning, the subject of Chapter 10, deals with the aftermath of disaster, and how to recover from it. No management can afford to ignore contingency planning.

Insurance is the most common way that organisations transfer risk to others. It is discussed in Chapter 11. Here as elsewhere, expert advice is needed before important decisions are taken. Data protection to safeguard personal information is important in the European scene, and legislation is promised soon in the UK. This has implications for every computer user which are considered in Chapter 12.

Finally there is a list of further reading, including some of the more important journals.

2 Security Principles

Computer systems are usually designed to perform certain functions and to provide essential or important services for an organisation. The systems may hold and process data vital to the organisation. Computer systems have in fact become an essential part of modern business and administration. We have come to expect good performance and behaviour of our computer systems. Today people expect these systems to work properly and be available when required. If we fail to get satisfactory service we are surprised or even annoyed. Designers and builders of systems are expected to look after these things. In a word, they are expected to provide security as part of the system design.

'Secure' may be defined as safe against attack or failure. This implies that there are some threats likely to upset or interfere with the system. Any system has to be implemented in a real world that is far from ideal. The system is surrounded by all kinds of threats. The environment is usually far from friendly.

Computer systems are part of corporate systems. As a rule we need to protect them from attack or failure, as part of the protection of the assets of the organisation. The steps taken to protect against attack or failure are security measures. They include validation checks on input data, and fire-resistant safes to protect media and the data that they contain. Data encryption on communication circuits, and personal badge-reader identity passes are other examples of security measures. We shall meet many others later on.

There are countless threats, some obvious, some undiscovered

11

until too late. Obviously, power supplies to a computer may fail from time to time especially in bad weather during winter. Programs may contain undiscovered bugs. Media, such as disks or tapes, may become corrupted. Staff may be careless or even criminal.

Threats are of two kinds: accidental and deliberate. A fire may start by accident, but arson is always a possibility that must be borne in mind. Deliberate threats always include an element of human intent. Defences against deliberate threats must take account of this. If your house has a good lock on the front door it may deter the thief. He may well move on to easier pickings elsewhere; or he may try the back door instead of the front one. In contrast, accidental threats never follow this pattern. Usually the accidental threats come from natural causes like the weather. The rain thunder cloud does not examine the condition of your roof before the storm. It pours down regardless. If your roof is leaky, too bad! On the other hand, unlike the thief, the rain won't hold off and try elsewhere for easier pickings if your roof is sound!

The distinction is especially important when considering people and security. People will by-pass security measures if they are allowed to do so. They will find ways round the defences unless you stop them.

We have to protect systems against attack or failure. The defences we use are called countermeasures. The lock on the door is a defence against the potential thief or intruder. How should one select appropriate defences? The problem is complex. Many countermeasures are usually available against any particular threat. Some will be more effective than others, but they will usually be the more expensive ones of course. For example, you can get all kinds of locks for your front door. You can have bolts or chains as well. There are special security doors designed for up-market property. How do you choose, since defences cost money?

Often defences are inconvenient as well. The door chain is an example of this. We tell granny to put the chain on, and check all callers, especially late at night. We know in our hearts that she only uses it when we are watching. How do you enforce security measures?

One thinks at first that all defences are a good thing. After all they contribute to better security, so they must be beneficial. This is not the case, in fact.

Consider a validation program designed to check input data to a program suite in a typical batch system. The program could be designed to check for all possible kinds or error. The design aim may not be achievable in any but the most trivial cases. Is such an aim in any event a worthwhile one? Checking for the more common types of error with good diagnostics may be a better aim. The cost of checking for very unlikely errors may be very high as a cumulative cost during system operation lifetime. It may be that the lower cost results from allowing the odd error from time to time.

Selection of fire precautions provides another example where the obvious solution is not necessarily the most appropriate. Computers and other modern high-value electronic equipment are very susceptible to damage by smoke, especially that from burning plastic. One of the most effective defences against the risk is to install smoke partitions to divide the area into smaller sections. One study showed that in cost/benefit terms this was likely to be the best way of spending available resources in large installations.

Cost is always a factor in selecting security measures. However, it is impossible to achieve perfect security even if resources are unlimited. Very high levels of protection can be achieved with proper management, but perfection is not attainable. In the Apollo missions to the moon, cost did not appear to be a severe limitation. Yet we have those immortal words from space 'Houston, we seem to have a slight problem!' The system was superb, and their recovery procedures worked, but despite all the care, they still had failures.

The choice of security measures is part of the process of risk management. Essentially one has to take into account all the possible significant threats that might affect the system. Then the available resources for security measures should be deployed on that set of countermeasures that will leave the smallest expected loss. In other words you should spend money on those measures that will give the greatest pay off. Risk management is discussed in more detail in Chapter 9.

When the defences fail and there is a breach of computer or system security there are three possible effects. There may be loss of availability, in that the system cannot provide service at the scheduled or expected time. Secondly there may be a breach of integrity, in that the system no longer performs properly. It does things that were not intended, or it does *not* do things that *were* intended. The processing is incorrect. The third possibility is a breach of confidentiality, where data is revealed to unauthorised people. Often this last kind of breach of security may pass unnoticed unless particular care is taken in the way data and media are controlled. Clearly a particular failure could cause effects under more than one of these three classes: *availability, integrity,* or *confidentiality*. A hardware failure might produce incorrect results of such seriousness that the machine would at once be taken out of service to rectify the fault.

No security programme produces perfect security. There will always be some residual risk of failure or other loss. There are two reasons for this. First the countermeasures may not be effective against all the threats that have been identified. Buildings with good fire detection systems are still destroyed from time to time; because, for example, there are some pyromaniacs about. The other point is that no risk analysis will identify all the threats that exist. This is especially the case for neighbourhood threats, and perhaps also for deliberate threats from terrorism or industrial action.

From time to time therefore the defences will fail and there will be a contingency (ie an unplanned interruption of data processing capability). The contingency may be a fire, a flood or some other calamity that stops one using the data processing system for some significant time. All well-managed data centres have back-up or contingency arrangements to cope with the situation. The subject of contingency planning is covered in Chapter 10. It is sometimes called *disaster planning* or *standby and recovery planning*.

In summary, security is about protection against attack or failure. No security programme can give absolute protection. A proper programme of risk analysis and management will ensure that available resources are deployed in the most effective manner. When a major breach of security does occur, there should be adequate plans to deal with it as a result of contingency planning.

3 Physical Security

GENERAL

The physical environment has enormous influence on the security of a computer system. Proper consideration of factors like location and building design and construction is vital, especially at the planning stage. It is much easier to eliminate potential security problems or minimise their effects at this stage. An existing building may have insolvable security problems.

Proven controls are missing in much current hardware and software. This means that physical security and administrative controls are often the only means of protecting DP resources. Many factors contribute to adequate physical security, and they tend to interact. For example, fire protection, access control and building construction are intimately linked. Sometimes measures taken to deal with one risk may make the problem of dealing with other risks more difficult. The conflict between the need to control access and provision of emergency exit routes is one example.

There are legal requirements in many countries on things like building construction, and fire protection measures. Computer users can benefit from experience in many other areas in matters of physical security. A wealth of information is available. Professional advice should be sought in cases of doubt.

LOCATION

A computer installation's location determines many of the risks that affect it. Any site is subject to many natural risks such as the weather and the stability (or otherwise) of the ground itself. The site is also subject to neighbourhood risks that result from mankind's activities nearby. The flight path to an international airport and certain chemical process plants are examples of possibly unwelcome neighbours. There are several hundred chemical plants, with potential for a Flixborough-type disaster within the UK.

There may be no opportunity to select a good site. The installation will have to use a site that the organisation has chosen for other reasons. The risks inherent in the location need to be assessed regardless of whether the computer is housed at an existing company location or in a specially selected site. These risks need to be reviewed from time to time.

NATURAL RISKS

Weather and its consequences are the most important natural risk for most locations. Wind, rain, snow and ice have obvious and often dramatic effects. Few sites are immune from the possibility of extreme weather conditions. Floods commonly follow heavy rainfall, but can be avoided by selecting a well drained site on high ground. Storm damage is commonplace from high winds, especially in areas subject to tropical storms. Britain, noted for a mild climate, also suffers from the weather, but on a reduced scale. Cooling towers at Ferrybridge power station, Yorkshire, collapsed during gusty winds in November 1965. The spire of the central tower at Lincolnshire Cathedral was blown down in an earlier storm. In May 1950 a tornado left a 160 kilometre trail of damage from Berkshire to Norfolk. Maximum wind speeds were estimated at about 100 metres per second (360 kilometres per hour).

The sheer impact of hurricane-force winds can do much physical damage by itself. Roofs can be lifted off and window glass broken. The flying debris can do more damage. Still worse is the risk of serious injury and death from such missiles. Narrow river valleys should be avoided. The destruction of Lynmouth by flash floods in August 1952 shows the type of site that should be avoided. Heavy rainfall on the surrounding moors was concentrated in the very narrow valley. The resulting torrents destroyed the centre of the town, and caused heavy casualties. Snow and ice can affect site access and transport. They may also disrupt services of all kinds, including water supply and air conditioning.

Lightning rarely causes structural damage to properly protected modern buildings, but it may affect electric power supplies to the site. There may be interruptions to the supply, or surges and transients which the equipment cannot tolerate. Communications lines can also be affected by lightning. Terminals may be damaged or destroyed unless the lines are protected. Lightning may cause misoperation of the computer system, resulting in system breaks or 'crashes'. One real-time hospital administration system was disrupted in this way 17 times in a single afternoon.

Flooding of the site is often caused by rain storms, possibly on higher ground further up a valley. Few storm water drainage systems can cope with extremes. High tides are another cause of flooding, especially during low-pressure storms.

Much of commercial London is vulnerable to this kind of flooding until the Thames barrage is completed. One of the clearing banks opened a new computer centre in the City with every possible refinement. Flooding of the basement standby generators was reported to be the major risk remaining. Canals and reservoirs can burst their banks, causing widespread floods. In some countries, landslip into large reservoirs has caused disasters. Vulnerable locations should be avoided.

Ground stability is vital, but often overlooked. Earthquakes and ground tremors are fairly common everywhere, though most frequent in the earthquake zones.

Landslip is very common, often associated with movement of ground water. It can affect a site by inundation with the slipped material, as at Aberfan in 1966. Landslip often blocks roads, rendering the site inaccessible. The slippage may rupture services such as water and gas pipes. The actual site may collapse. This is common on cliff-top locations and valley sides. The ground may be affected by subsidence from mining activities or brine pumping in salt-producing regions. Appropriate measures at the building design stage can minimise or eliminate many of the problems associated with any particular site.

NEIGHBOURHOOD RISKS

Other people's activities in the neighbourhood pose further risks. Some are obvious. The flight path to a major airport has an increased risk of an aircraft disaster. A neighbouring motorway, particularly if elevated, increases the possibility of a heavy vehicle accident. This might release toxic gases or result in an explosion. Other risks are hidden. There may be a hazardous process in a neighbouring factory.

The past and future activities nearby should be considered. Obsolete mine workings or other extraction industries may have left hidden shafts. Salt extraction by brine pumping caused unpredictable subsidence near Northwich in Cheshire. Building work or heavy industry nearby may introduce other risks, such as vibration from pile driving, or dust from cement silos. The chemical industries often involve hazardous processes or toxic substances. Even the associated transport may introduce risks of fire, explosion or toxic fumes following an accident.

Public services are vital to any installation. These include electricity, gas, water, drainage and sewerage, telecommunications and transport. Good road access is needed not only for normal business but also for emergencies. It is essential for fire services and ambulances. If possible the site should be approachable from two different directions. Vital services like power and communication circuits should be duplicated via different routes. Road works can easily disrupt them.

Sociopolitical risks are particularly difficult to deal with. Vandals, demonstrators, rioters, terrorists can all take actions that may disrupt operations, or even destroy the installation. An unobtrusive site in a good neighbourhood is a good first line of defence against these risks.

The choice of a suitable location can reduce many of the physical risks. The chosen site may have important advantages that override its otherwise serious physical risks. A balanced view must be taken. There may be no choice of site, especially with an existing operation, and some risks will be unavoidable.

It may be economic to introduce appropriate countermeasures

in the building design layout and construction rather than to use an expensive but safe site.

Localities change their character as development occurs. New risks arise and old ones disappear. Competent management is alive to such changes and takes account of them. If you don't know what the place is coming to, then you should!

BUILDING CONSTRUCTION AND DESIGN

The building housing the installation makes a most important contribution to its security. It provides accommodation for the computer system, personnel and ancillary services. Failures or shortcomings in the design will affect the installation in all sorts of ways.

The building may be purpose-built or adapted from other accommodation. The computer system may be the only activity on the site or it may be part of a much larger complex activity.

Conventional construction techniques and materials should be used. This eliminates unknown risks from new untried methods. Many modern materials produce toxic fumes in a fire, and some assist the spread of flames. The structure should be fire-resistant. Sound construction can eliminate many problems.

The layout and design should so far as possible eliminate hiding places. A smooth exterior is desirable to minimise the possibility of concealing explosive or incendiary devices.

If the building is shared then proper segregation is needed both vertically and horizontally. The computer area should be separated from other activities by fire- and flood-resistant walls or partitions. These must extend through any floor voids and false ceilings. The integrity of these walls must be maintained through the building's lifetime. Quite small holes for cables or other services may make them useless, and reduce the effectiveness of fire quenching by gas flooding.

Wherever possible all facilities should be located above ground level to avoid danger from flooding, backed-up sewers, or fire-fighting measures. Underground areas must be provided with floor drains, pumps or other protection.

All penetrations of fire walls and floor slabs need adequate fire stopping. Openings made for cables, ducts and pipes must be sealed with materials adequate to resist passage of heat, flame, smoke and water. Such openings may be breached during modifications to the installation, when, for example, new equipment and cables are introduced. The installation engineers may leave openings unstopped, and regular inspections are needed to ensure that perimeter and other walls have not been breached.

In multi-storey buildings the floor above the computer must protect against spillage, or other water leakage.

The routes for services such as gas and water need selecting with care. Things like header tanks for heating systems ought to be eliminated from the computer area. One often sees water pipes and other services in false ceilings.

Sufficient space must be allowed for expansion of the installation, both in equipment and manpower. There should be ample and convenient storage areas. Problems of floor loading must not be overlooked, especially for media libraries and stationery storage.

Layout is important. There should be as few doors as possible to the exterior. The number of doors, windows, ventilation inlets and outlets should be limited. Their accessibility to vandals must be considered. Quite a small hole is sufficient to introduce an incendiary device, especially by night.

It is an advantage to have a perimeter fence or even a low wall that is clear of the walls of the building. This is better than having the building fronting directly onto the street or other public places. The zone between the building and the street is then subject to control. Anyone within it can be challenged, which is not the case if they are simply loitering suspiciously on the street.

The existence or location of the computer installation should not be obvious or made apparent to outsiders. Direction signs and descriptive nameplates are best avoided, except for 'Way Out' and 'emergency exit' signs. There is no point in helping intruders. For similar reasons, plans of the building should not be displayed in entrances and corridors. Those that are needed for fire protection purposes should be within a reception office, not on public view.

Emergency evacuation routes and procedures need planning carefully. Ideally, the way in should also be the way out. This is most natural, and it is self-maintaining. Passages and routes that are rarely used tend to get blocked. People tend to go out by the entrance route, rather than by the perhaps rarely used emergency exit.

Bomb threats present other problems. Should one evacuate or not? Staff gathered at an assembly point are possibly more vulnerable to terrorists than they would be dispersed round the installation. A protected assembly area within a perimeter fence may be less dangerous than a public street. Local advice should be sought from the police.

ELECTRIC POWER SUPPLY

We take electric power for granted. No computer can operate without it, but many less obvious services and ancillaries are totally dependent upon continued electricity supply. Lighting, lifts and alarm systems, as well as air conditioning, will fail without it. Public electricity supplies are generally very reliable indeed. Except in outlying areas the supply rarely fails by accident. Most major consumers can arrange to have two independent supply routes, so that there is fall-back if one should fail. The public supply will fail for various reasons, including accidental damage to supply lines or substations, industrial action, load shedding at peak periods.

Supplies may be interrupted over a wide area, so that duplicate local feeds may both be useless. The main UK grid system failed in August 1981, leaving large parts of the South without any kind of power for several hours. This was most unusual, however.

Disturbances in the supply are far more common. Voltage and frequency reductions are often made to shed load in winter. There are transient disturbances caused by lightning strikes and plant failures. Other nearby plant such as lifts and other machinery may introduce transients on the supply, or produce harmonics.

The equipment can be isolated from the short fluctuations by using a motor-alternator set. This acts as a buffer between the mains and the computer power supply units, and can cope with disturbances lasting up to 100 milliseconds. A flywheel included in the motor alternator can increase this to several seconds.

Various forms of uninterruptable power supply are available, which take over the load automatically to allow controlled shutdown of the installation.

Diesel generator and gas turbine sets are also widely available. These can provide power for as long as the fuel supplies can be maintained. They can be arranged with automatic start-up gear. A standby generator with battery-supported uninterruptable power supply can maintain supplies indefinitely. The disadvantage is the very high capital cost of such equipment, to say nothing of its maintenance. Any form of standby power needs regular running and maintenance to keep it in working order.

Adequate arrangements for fuel supplies must be made. It may be possible to hire a road tanker vehicle temporarily for emergencies provided prior arrangements are made. Fuel pumping must be independent of the public electricity supply. A case was reported from New York where the fuel tanks were in the basement of the skyscraper. The pumps to the diesel generators were supplied from the mains.

In most installations standby power will prove to be too expensive. Standby emergency lighting is always necessary, but can be quite cheap, since quite low levels of lighting are adequate for escape. The normal arrangement is a battery system coupled with an automatic mains charger. Such systems should be switched on every week for several hours.

One or two large electric torches or lanterns should be provided at known locations like the main console and data reception desk.

The standby power supply must be large enough to handle the peak load of the installation, including the air conditioning plant. Some peripherals might be switched off in an emergency to reduce the loading, but calculations may show that this has only marginal effects on the total load of the installation.

Power supply equipment and other plant should be segregated from the computer equipment. Smoke and fire can arise from plant failure. The smoke from PVC fires is corrosive, and can seriously damage other equipment.

Electrical plant and cabling should be properly protected from unqualified personnel. Changes in the installation ('enhancements') often need changes in cabling. Old redundant cables should be removed, and all cable runs should be kept tidy. Layout drawings of cable arrangements should be properly updated. All rubbish must be removed from under-floor spaces.

AIR CONDITIONING

Small computers are often installed in an ordinary office. Larger machines dissipate so much heat that ventilation is needed simply to maintain tolerable summer working conditions for staff. For mainframes the manufacturer will stipulate the environment required. The requirements should be checked before the contract is signed. Humidity and temperature must be controlled, and a dust-free atmosphere maintained. This can be achieved only with air conditioning plants.

Typical conditions are a temperature of 21°C ± 2°C (70°F ± 3°F) and relative humidity of 50% ± 5%. If no magnetic media devices are installed these conditions may be relaxed. A typical air conditioning plant recirculates some of the air and introduces a continuous supply of clean filtered air at the correct temperature and humidity. Some air is exhausted to the outside. Usually the air conditioned space is maintained at a slight positive pressure, so that any leaks are clean air passing outwards, rather than dirty air passing inwards. The air that is lost and the air conditioning cooling plant have to remove the waste heat from the computer. Most of the electrical energy supplied will be converted to heat. If the plant should fail then the room temperature will quickly rise, putting the equipment at risk. The temperature of the air inside a working computer is always higher than that outside the cabinets. The difference in temperature is necessary to clear away the waste heat.

Variations in conditions can lead to overheating of components, moisture precipitation (especially if the equipment is switched off) and to build-up of excess static electricity. Too dry an atmosphere may cause curling of cards and magnetic tape. Stationery may distort in extreme conditions and be unusable.

Dust can be introduced if air conditioning plant is not properly maintained. Faulty air conditioning can cause all kinds of intermittent problems on magnetic tape and disk equipment. Staff can introduce dust on shoes and clothing. Special mats and floor coverings are available to reduce these problems. Appropriate floor treatment can reduce static electricity problems.

Air conditioning for a computer installation is best if it is totally separate from any other air conditioning system. Refrigeration compressors, cooling towers and so on may be common to other systems if necessary. In such cases the distribution of conditioned air to the computer and its ancillaries must be totally separate from that used elsewhere. Moreover the ducts supplying other areas must not pass through the computer area.

All duct insulation and linings, including vapour barriers, should be non-combustible.

Air conditioning equipment is normally linked to fire alarm systems. Clearly the supply of air must be stopped if there is a fire, or it will simply fan the flames.

Every precaution is needed to prevent ingress of smoke from fires elsewhere in the building. Almost insignificant amounts of smoke can contaminate disk heads, and result in reading faults or worse. There are many cases where a small cable fire has produced corrosive smoke from burning PVC. The air conditioning has ducted it into a computer room. Computers have been written off by the insurers as a total loss for this reason.

Some installations have a carbon dioxide or Halon gas flooding system for extinguishing fires. The ventilation or air conditioning system must be capable of clearing the extinguishing agent from the flooded spaces after the fire has been suppressed. Special ventilation may be needed for floor and ceiling voids. Air conditioning systems need proper maintenance. Ducting may deteriorate and introduce contaminants (rust, paint particles, etc) after many years' use.

ACCESS CONTROL

Normal entry and exit should be through one properly controlled and monitored access point. Nobody and nothing should be allowed in the computer room unless their presence is essential at the time. A proper access control system should be flexible so that it can meet changing needs. Ideally it should maintain records of who was present at all times, so that there is a proper audit record.

As a point of interest most systems allow or deny passage through the gate. They do not monitor actual presence within the controlled area. The layout of the installation should be arranged to minimise traffic flow between the different controlled areas.

Many installations have serious access control deficiencies and only token protection. Strong management leadership is needed to establish and maintain adequate physical access control.

Clearly the imposition of any sort of access control might be taken to imply a lack of trust. It might be resented by staff, and produce hostility. The system might also be seen to offer protection for the staff against threats from intruders (thieves or terrorists) and make staff feel more secure. No matter what method is selected it must be effective. Management should explain clearly why the system is there, how it is to be used, and what penalties will follow non-compliance. A token system should not be tolerated. The selected system should cause minimum inconvenience consistent with the level of security needed.

The three basic ways of restricting access and controlling it are those using people, those using mechanical locks, and the various electronic systems.

Ultimately all systems depend for success upon people, but conventionally we think of the people systems as those systems using receptionists or security guards. They can challenge strangers and call for help if necessary. Procedures must be established so that the person on duty has instructions for all eventualities, and can summon help unobtrusively. The person should be protected by a security fence or window from physical attack. Access to the rest of the building should be prevented by a self-closing door with an electrically operated remote latch. A turnstile is even better.

If a security officer is employed then he will need some means of identifying authorised staff. This may be a list, but it is more than likely that badges or passes will have to be issued. Passes should be checked at each entry. The routine production of a valid pass not only identifies the authorised individual, but also ensures that the pass has not been lost or stolen. Passes should include a colour photograph and specimen signature, so that the guard or receptionist can relate the face and the pass. Security staff may be reluctant to ask senior management to produce a pass. Such people should set an example and raise questions if they are *not* asked to produce identification.

Badges should be worn prominently either on a clip or neck-chain. Clearly visible badges help staff to identify strangers – who will not have a badge – and assist in checking that the badges have not been lost or mislaid. Some organisations 'badge' visitors whilst employees are unbadged. This is totally illogical. If badges are used they should be worn prominently. Visitors should be identified with distinctive badges and accompanied at all times. Staff should be required to challenge anyone without a badge and all un-escorted visitors. Moreover they should be trained to call in security or other responsible staff as a matter of course on all such challenges. Most intruders will have a plausible story ready to meet a challenge ('I've come to see the contractor') and will trade upon the courtesy and helpfulness of the average staff member.

People systems are not effective when traffic is high. The security officer is easily diverted if large numbers are present. He is also sometimes unpredictable, and unaware of changes. Sometimes security staff are expected to perform other tasks that divert them from their proper duties.

People are very expensive as a means of checking other people. Frequently breaches of security pass unnoticed. People are much better employed in checking that other systems are properly used.

Mechanical Locks

Conventional locks and keys are quite useful for small installations, and especially for controlling access to places like store rooms and plant rooms. People will accept the inconvenience of unlocking and locking doors that are not in constant use. They are tolerable for two or three times a day, but not for 10 or 20 times a day. As traffic increases, doors will be propped or wedged open, and locks will be taped-over to prevent them latching. This happens even with fire check doors designed to protect people.

Most keys are easily duplicated, and they are frequently lost or mislaid. Staff tend to put them in pockets. They then go off duty taking the store room key, leaving colleagues without access. Fire data safes usually have keys, but their general utility is doubtful if several people need to use the same lock.

If keys are used there should be a properly controlled key board. One good design uses coloured key fobs that match colour patches around the correct hook. A glance is sufficient to see that all keys are in place and correctly located.

Electronic Systems

Card locks and other electronic systems are now very common. Often they are combined with key pads and time clocks to control or deny passage. Several kinds of card are in use. Optical and magnetic encoding is used to record an identification on the card. The card is inserted in a slot alongside the controlled door. The card reader releases the door latch for a predetermined time if passage is authorised. Systems can be arranged so that different cards are allowed access at various periods. Some cards might give 24-hour access, whereas others used say by early morning staff might be allowed access only between 7.00 and 9.00 a.m. Again installations may have several controlled doors, and the system can be programmed so that individual cards are given access to particular sets of doors, possibly even at different times. Modern systems use microcomputers. This allows programming of quite complex arrangements. Lost or mislaid cards can be cancelled. Individuals can be given temporary access to special areas, without the need to modify the card in any way.

Card systems give good control of external doors. For this use they should be combined with a keypad. The individual then needs to possess the card and to know the correct key sequence before gaining access. This minimises danger from misuse of lost cards. The system may require a different key sequence for each individual. There is then little danger from people writing the number on the wall.

Card keys can be combined with identification badges, including photograph and other details. An advantage here is that the key looks less like a key. The casual finder might think it is only a badge.

Pass-back of cards is less of a problem when the card is also a badge that must be worn. Follow-through is a problem on any unmanned system. An unauthorised person can follow someone else without actually using a card. Turnstiles are one way of overcoming this; they are effective even at very high traffic densities, such as ticket barriers on the underground. Doors can be linked to an alarm that sounds if the door is not closed promptly. This discourages people from holding the door open for others to follow. It also gives warning if the door sticks for some reason.

Electronic locks can be by-passed as effectively as mechanical ones. Cards can be taped into reader slots, and codes can be written on walls. Even when they are operating correctly, systems cannot detect unauthorised entry. At best they control passage. They certainly do not monitor presence within the controlled areas. The best systems are able to log all usage so that it can be monitored. Such monitoring might disclose unauthorised or irregular out-of-hours activity. This might indicate need for further investigation by audit or security staff.

Automatic Access Control

Card systems and mechanical locks are not tolerable for use more than a few times a day. A layout that forces people to pass a barrier frequently is poorly designed, incidentally.

A system which overcomes the problem of inconvenience is one in which the operation of the security device (lock, barrier, alarm, etc) is controlled by coded signals emitted by a small electronic transmitter. This transmitter is carried in a pocket or clipped to a waistband or dress by those authorised to enter any of the protected areas under the control of the system.

Authorised entrants to the protected areas collect their transmitters in the morning from the charging device in which they have been stored overnight. They then keep the transmitter on their person until they leave at the end of the day.

When someone approaches a controlled area, the electronic system automatically checks whether the would-be entrant has an appropriate transmitter which authorises entry to that particular area. The system then permits immediate free passage by releasing the door lock, activating the automatic door-opening mechanism, suppressing the alarm or taking whatever other action is necessary to permit unrestricted entry. With no transmitter or an incorrect transmitter, access remains firmly barred. The authorised user is not required to take any action and yet has complete freedom of movement. The unauthorised user is barred; the intruder who attempts to follow can be detected, and alarms actuated.

Detection devices can be installed to prevent transmitters being inadvertently or deliberately removed from the premises, although any transmitter which is not returned to the special charging device would be inoperable the next day.

Systems of this type are most appropriate where frequent access to controlled areas is required by authorised personnel, and are best installed at the building stage.

Out-of-Hours Control

Out of normal hours it is common for operations staff to work in small groups, often in an otherwise empty building. Such staff must be trained to treat all callers with suspicion. Even when callers are expected (like courier services or maintenance engineers) identities must be checked before the door is opened. Unexpected visitors should never be admitted. Good external lighting and peep holes in doors are essential. Cases are on record where operations staff have been overpowered by thieves seeking access to premises through a computer room back door.

EAVESDROPPING

Access can be gained to information without actual entry to the premises. Information being processed, transmitted or displayed is vulnerable to modern techniques of surveillance.

The equipment or installation can be 'bugged' by incorporating transmitters within it. Similar radio bugs can be attached to a telephone in a few moments. They can be activated remotely by telephone from anywhere in the world. Wiretapping is possible on communication lines either within the building or outside on the circuits to the exchange.

Many electronic devices emit radio signals that can be picked up at reasonable distances with fairly simple equipment. For example, most personal computers using video displays can be monitored at several hundred feet with relatively simple equipment. The monitor display will replicate the display on the personal computer. This would be quite simple within many office complexes. Note though that the observer could be in a car or van in the street.

The greatest hazard is probably from people attaching terminals into multi-access systems. It is surprising how many city centre telephone numbers give direct access to modems, and sensible responses on terminal devices. Display terminals should always be sited facing away from windows. Photographic and other optical gear is available to allow observation and recording from several hundred metres. A 1400 mm lens, with sufficient definition for this purpose, can be obtained.

Encryption

The classic defence against eavesdropping is encryption or scrambling. One may want to protect the data itself. It may be sensitive for commercial reasons or reasons of personal privacy (data protection). Encryption also allows one to disguise the fact that important information is transmitted at intervals. One can transmit random encrypted messages in between the important ones. The observer cannot identify the significant information without decrypting the whole stream.

Encryption can also be used to verify that messages are genuine, and to protect passwords stored in a computer. Many products are now available to facilitate use of encryption techniques.

ELECTROMAGNETIC AND OTHER RADIATION

Magnets near or in contact with magnetic media can cause serious damage. All kinds of magnets should be excluded from areas where media are handled or stored. Magnets have no effects on media from distances exceeding 10-15 cm. The main thing is to avoid accidental contact with things like magnetic catches on cupboard doors. Magnets are often used on metal clipboards by contractors.

Portable transceivers ('walkie talkies') can interfere with nearby computing equipment. Tests should be made before using them to check that there is no effect.

Radiation and radioactive particles are not a threat to data processing installations. Unexposed film might be affected. The magnetic fields associated with X-rays or atomic radiation are insignificant. They would not affect magnetic media.

Radio and radar can affect equipment. High signal strengths (5 volts/metre or more) are needed. These are only likely if the antenna is visible and pointing directly through a window. Simple aluminium mesh at windows will eliminate the problem in normal buildings. Interference may introduce spurious signals into the computer circuits resulting in errors or misoperation. Radar will not affect magnetic media unless the media are very close to the transmitting antenna.

4 Fire Protection

Fire is usually the most serious risk faced by any organisation. One problem with fire is that although we are aware of its dangers we ignore them. Fire precautions are often treated with contempt.

It used to be said that computers had a low inherent fire risk. This is probably true, but computers have to be operated by people in buildings. The actual incidence of fires in computer centres is probably much the same as the incidence in offices generally. Most of us know of small fires in or near computer rooms. About 10 per cent of small fires grow into big fires. A big fire in a computer centre or even a small one nearby can cause very big property loss. The consequential loss for the organisation could also be very large.

Fire and smoke also represent grave risks for people. Most countries have laws about fire protection, that attempt to enforce minimum standards. The Fire Precautions Act 1971 is an example.

Insurers are very concerned about fire losses because of their high potential cost. Over the years they have accumulated a great deal of experience. Special recommendations have been developed for data processing installations. These are revised from time to time as new knowledge comes to light.

The Fire Offices' Committee issues rules for the Protection of Computer Installations against fire. There is also a draft British Standard Code of Practice on the subject. The US Department of Commerce has issued a Standard Practice for the Fire Protection of Essential Electronic Equipment Operations. Other examples abound. Different countries have different standards, but a great deal is based on common experience.

Computer rooms constructed some years ago are unlikely to meet present-day recommendations. It is certainly worth checking an installation for conformity with current practice.

CONSTRUCTION

Fire in some other area could spread to involve a computer, and heat, smoke and water reaching it can cause costly damage. Fire protection codes stress the importance of construction and materials in preventing the spread of fire. It is best if data processing can be done in a building reserved exclusively for the purpose. If the building must be shared with other activities, then the DP areas must be separated from other areas by walls and floors made of non-combustible materials. The walls must extend from true floor to true ceiling. The required fire resistance of these walls and floors varies according to what activities are carried out in the other parts of the building. As little as one hour may suffice for offices, rising to four hours for activities like furniture warehousing, where there is a heavy loading of combustible materials.

Unnecessary openings in the walls and floors should be avoided. Those that are essential should be protected to retain the same standards of fire resistance as the walls. This might be a self-closing door with one hour's fire resistance in offices.

In high fire load situations such a door would be supplemented by a roller shutter of two hours' resistance held open by fusible links. Expert advice is needed at the design stage.

All openings like those for cables and pipes in fire separation walls and floors should be made good with fire stopping material of the same fire resistance. There is a tendency to leave openings unstopped so that more cables can be added later. This should be resisted.

Floors above computer rooms should be waterproof, and other precautions should be taken to prevent water entering the area. Plastic sheets should be ready to hand to cover equipment in case of leaks from above. False floors should be supported on non-combustible materials of adequate strength. The actual floor material should be designed to resist a fire in the floor void, possibly by lining the underside with non-combustible material.

All materials used in linings and for suspended ceilings should be non-combustible. They should not produce dust, or corrosive or toxic fumes when heated.

Suspended ceilings are almost universal in computer rooms. They contain air conditioning ducts, power cables and lighting equipment. The voids in such ceilings provide concealed spaces in which fire could develop. Such a fire is difficult to locate and without adequate detection equipment it could spread. The materials used in ceiling fittings should be carefully considered. Ventilation grills, light diffusers and decorations may all be hazardous unless their materials have self-extinguishing properties.

Within the DP area there should be separation of the various activities by non-combustible partitions from true floor to true ceiling. Such partitions will help to stop the spread of smoke and fire within the installation. Self-closing doors with at least one hour's fire resistance should be used in such partitions. Data preparation and working stationery stores are best separated in this way. When an installation contains more than one computer system they should be separated by fire-resisting partitions. Many DP installations are designed without windows. Precautions may be needed to prevent accumulation of heat and smoke, and to ensure easy staff escape and access for fire-fighting personnel.

AIR CONDITIONING

The air conditioning supply to computer rooms must be separate from any other system. Otherwise there is grave risk of carrying heat, smoke and fire into the computer area from fires elsewhere. For the same reason the ducting supplying other areas must not pass through the computer area unless it is enclosed in a fire-resistant stack. All ducts and trunking should incorporate automatic fire shutters or dampers at the segregation walls and floors. These are normally held open by a fusible link or an electromagnetic device.

Combustible materials should not be used in the ducting, linings, acoustic treatments or insulation. Air filters should be non-combustible and they should be cleaned regularly to remove fluff and other combustible materials.

There should be provision for stopping the fans if there is a fire in the installation. This may be linked to automatic fire detection equipment, but there should be manual switch-off as well.

Ducts and trunking intended for smoke extraction should not have fire dampers that can be closed when the smoke extracting system is in operation.

POWER DISCONNECTION

Every installation should have an emergency 'knock off' button that can be used in emergency to disconnect the power supply to the computer, the air conditioning and main power except lighting. It should be sited near the main exit. Duplicate buttons may be needed on a large site with other exits. Such buttons should be shrouded to prevent accidental use.

It may also be necessary to have a special 'fireman's switch' at or near the main entrance marked FIRE EMERGENCY SWITCH.

There may be time to power-down in a sensible sequence, especially if the fire is in another part of the site. An appropriate sequence should be devised that gives the best safeguard to data and equipment without putting staff at risk. The switch-off sequence might not be the one that would be used in ordinary conditions. The manufacturer may be able to offer useful advice as to the best procedure.

EVACUATION AND ESCAPE

A very real danger in modern conditions is the wide use of plastics, not only in upholstery and other furniture, but in almost everything else. Many plastics produce toxic or corrosive fumes when heated. The fumes can be lethal long before there is any flame. People may have only 60-90 seconds to escape from such conditions. There is a general lack of awareness of the problem, and our attitudes do not match up to the realities. Many far-sighted organisations have changed their fire precaution instructions in recent years, and now stress the need to evacuate. Getting people out quickly makes sense. (It could be argued that fighting fires is not a job for untrained people.) If everyone is accounted for, the fire brigade can fight the fire.

There is no room for doubt here. Either everyone is accounted for or they are not. If someone might still be in the building, the fire brigade will be put to unnecessary risk seeking them out. Whatever access control method is used must provide confirmation that everyone is accounted for.

Escape routes are vital. They should be used regularly to make sure that they are not obstructed. Remember people habitually go out the same way that they came in – if they can find it. The entrance route may be a very poor or even dangerous exit route in an emergency. Train people to use the safe emergency routes to spread the load off the main staircases.

Plans for escape should consider visitors and contractors who may be unfamiliar with the building.

Clear signs and emergency lighting are vital. Places like store rooms, plant rooms, and other dead ends should be kept locked. Even better they should be labelled 'No exit this way' so that there is no doubt.

STORAGE MEDIA

Most materials used to store information will burn. Once ignited they will often burn vigorously. Magnetic tape and tape reels, tape and disk canisters are fairly combustible, and will certainly distort under heat. Although disks will not burn they will be rendered useless. Even disks mounted in inoperative drive units may be made unreadable as a consequence of fire.

Paper burns readily and a fire in a paper store may cause disaster from smoke contamination. Media should be kept away from the computer room in a separate area. Vital records should be protected in special fire-resistant safes or vaults. These records should be duplicated in off-site storage so that recovery is possible when the fire safes are inaccessible. It might be several days before safes can be located in the aftermath of a big fire. In such circumstances the makers or other specialists should be asked to open the safe. There are cases where salvage teams have attempted to open such safes on site with torches. Their actions have destroyed media that had withstood the original fire in the security of the safe.

FIRE DETECTION AND ALARMS

Automatic fire detection equipment should be installed in spaces where fire could develop or spread undetected. Floor voids and store rooms will need detectors even in an installation that is always manned. (Most installations are not manned for 365 days a year even if 24 hour shifts are operated. They will need automatic detectors.)

Detectors need to operate at the earliest possible stage of a fire. High-value computer equipment is sensitive to damage by even a small fire. This means that a high concentration of detectors need to be used. A high detector density should enable the smallest fire to be detected without the danger of false alarms.

The selection of suitable detectors and their positions needs careful consideration. Each installation is a special case and experts should be entrusted with the design.

Smoke detectors are widely used. They work on two different principles. One is the ionisation chamber principle and the other the optical scattering principle. They are effective with different types of fire at different stages. The optical scatter detector works because smoke particles scatter light. A smouldering PVC cable produces dense white smoke which is readily detected by this device. The ionisation detector is insensitive to this kind of fire. However, it will detect a fire in a waste paper basket before you can see any smoke at all.

The British Standard draft code of practice recommends an equal mixture of both types. It also recommends the density of detectors that should be used. In a typical computer room three metres high at least one detector is needed for every 25 square metres; one detector is stipulated for every 25 to 40 square metres. A higher density of detectors is needed if such spaces are ventilated because of the dilution effects. One detector to each 10 to 30 square metres is suggested.

If fire breaks out, the alarms sound. Fire bells should be distinct from any other kind of warning or signal. Computer rooms often have quite high noise levels, and alarms suitable for a quiet office may be quite inaudible. The fire brigade should be called to all fires, no matter how small.

A direct link to call the fire brigade is very desirable. Calling the brigade twice or even ten times is better than no call. Unless procedures are laid down the call may not be made, and vital minutes will be lost. The Maltings Concert Hall at Snape in Suffolk burned for 30 minutes before a crowd of holiday makers. No one raised the alarm. At the Summerlands disaster in the Isle of Man, the brigade was not called for 35 minutes after the outbreak was noticed. Dozens of similar cases could be cited from all parts of the world.

The fire brigade usually respond swiftly to any call. At one installation a small fire resulted from some building activities (always risky). The fire was quickly extinguished, but we called the brigade to ask them to inspect. Almost at once the site was invaded by firemen – dozens of them. As the senior officer remarked 'If you are a five-appliance site you get five appliances. We can always send them back if they are not needed.'

FIRE QUENCHING

Portable extinguishers, sprinkler systems and automatic gas flooding systems are all used in data processing installations. Portable carbon dioxide or Halon extinguishers should be provided near equipment.

Water extinguishers and hose reels are needed where lots of paper is handled, and should be available immediately outside computer rooms. Often overlooked are heat-resisting gloves or cloths to help remove overheated components. A floor lifter should be at hand where modular false floors are installed to give access to cables. Fire blankets should also be provided, preferably suspended in a cylinder clearly visible to all personnel.

Hand extinguishers are provided everywhere these days, but how many people are trained how to use them? When people are frightened they do all kinds of foolish things. They may pick up extinguishers and discharge them without going anywhere near the flames.

The proper way of handling extinguishers is not obvious to the layman and regular training is needed. One woman discovered a fire in a photocopying machine. She seized the BCF extinguisher from the wall, but couldn't read the instructions without her glasses! Many people are wary of the equipment because they do not understand it. At a training session for operations staff the local fire service demonstrated the use of our two kinds of extinguisher. They then invited each person to have a go. Over half the staff refused to do so.

Timid people using an extinguisher for the first time may be startled by the force and noise. They may simply drop the thing and run for dear life.

A common folly is to throw the extinguisher on the fire. The case of a security guard with clear leadership qualities is on record. He organised a chain of people while waiting for the arrival of the brigade. They passed the extinguishers to him. He in turn threw them into the fire, one by one. Later he complained bitterly that the extinguishers not only failed to put out the fire, but that not one of them went off.

Gas Flooding Systems

Carbon dioxide and Halon gas are very effective fire extinguishing agents. Gas flooding systems are designed to flood a computer room or other space with the gas, and thus put out a fire. The gas can reach every nook and cranny of the protected space. It is especially useful for confined spaces like floor and ceiling voids, where some parts may be difficult to reach with portable equipment. Halon systems are sometimes used to protect individual cabinets.

Something like thirty per cent by volume of carbon dioxide (CO_2) will extinguish almost any fire in a computer room, from a waste paper basket to a petrol bomb. A CO_2 flooding system linked to fire detectors would provide an ideal system. There is a snag. It takes 30 per cent CO_2 to put out a fire, but only ten per cent to knock out the staff. All CO_2 systems should be locked-off when people are present. Put to automatic at night or when the premises are unoccupied, they provide ideal protection. The gas is cheap and it works extremely well. However, it has an element of danger and other gases known as Halons are replacing it in many applications.

The US Army Halon-numbering system is widely used for identifying halogenated agents. The first digit of the Halon number represents the number of carbon atoms, the second digit the number of fluorine atoms, the third the number of chlorine atoms, and the fourth bromine; the optional fifth represents the number of iodine atoms. Hence bromo tri fluoromethane is known as Halon 1301. (The other Halon used as an extinguishing agent is BCF/Halon 1211 Bromochloro di fluoromethane.)

Halon 1301 is slightly less toxic than Halon 1211. Halons will extinguish fire in much lower concentration than is needed with carbon dioxide. They can be arranged to flood the whole area, or floor or ceiling voids, or just individual cabinets. Only five per cent by volume of Halon is needed to extinguish a typical fire.

The gas is quite expensive, but the cost of discharging the system may be much less than the likely loss from a fire. If you can put out a fire with a small extinguisher and minimum damage, that is the cheapest way.

There are Health and Safety requirements whenever gas flooding systems are installed. Suitable warning notices are required at all entrances. Lock-offs have been required whenever people are present, so that the gas cannot be discharged automatically. Provision should be made to allow manual operation from outside the area after people have left. When the area is unmanned the discharge system should be set to automatic.

It is possible that automatic systems might be permitted in occupied rooms provided there is a time delay after the fire alarm to allow people to escape.

Sprinkler Systems

Sprinkler systems are becoming more common in computer rooms. They have long been popular in the United States. Their primary purpose is to provide disaster protection in major fires. They are an excellent long stop when everything else has failed. Much slower to respond than gas systems, it takes a big fire to operate a sprinkler. Sprinklers are designed to stop a fire progressing into a disaster involving total destruction. A sprinkler system often puts out a major fire with only one sprinkler operating. Damage will be much greater as a rule than it would be if the fire had been extinguished at an early stage. However, a twenty thousand pound loss is much better than total destruction of a ten million pound installation.

STAFF

Staff responsibilities must be clearly defined. Fire instructions and planning should emphasise that people matter most. (The most expensive installation can be rebuilt, in time.)

Operations staff often have to work in small groups of two or three at night. They lack the support of other people that their day shift colleagues enjoy. I still find managements who allow one person to operate a machine alone in an empty building. Quite apart from the asset security implications, this situation might be a disaster for the individual concerned. As well as the fire risks there is danger from machinery and electric shock.

There should be a clear policy on smoking. A legitimate place and time for smoking should be provided; whatever the rules, some people will smoke. Food and drink should be confined to the same areas. Cigarettes and coffee go together all too easily. (Just check the debris you find under a big piece of computer room equipment such as a disk drive when it is shifted!) Ash trays or sand bins should be provided outside the installation.

End of day and end of week procedures are an essential part of fire precautions. Closing down plant and equipment, and switch-over from manual to automatic need to be covered. Other aspects are the movement of records and media to safe storage. Procedures for handover of keys and locking doors must be specified. Maintaining good practice here demands vigilance from management.

5 People and Organisation

The people involved in a computer system are the key to all security measures. It is these people – management, systems analysts, programmers, designers, operators, maintenance engineers, contractors, cleaners, users, etc – who must be relied upon to maintain and operate effective security measures. The most vulnerable aspect in maintaining the security of the system is almost always the people who must necessarily be involved. The importance of personnel in maintaining security cannot be over-emphasised.

Personnel policies should take security needs into account, starting at recruitment and continuing right through to termination or retirement.

No system can be made absolutely safe from the consequences of people's inadvertent mistakes, whether these are due to inexperience or to poor training. More worrying, but possibly receiving less attention, is the threat from malicious acts or subversion. Designers of military and defence systems take this threat seriously. So should their colleagues in business and administration, where the threat can have important, even catastrophic, consequences for the organisation.

Personnel aspects of security can be classified in two ways. There is first the obvious one of protecting systems from personnel, from their accidental or deliberate acts or omissions that might otherwise cause a security breach. Computer fraud is obviously a 'people' problem. Most cases involve insiders, so that employee honesty is very important. The other aspect of security is protection of personnel, not only in normal conditions but in contingency or disaster situations. Many countries now have legislation to protect the health and safety of employees. An example is the UK Health and Safety at Work Act 1974, which places obligations on all those involved in an enterprise. Fire precaution instructions are an example where expert thinking is changing. The emphasis now is very much more on protection of people. Evacuation from premises is seen as the most urgent requirement if a fire should break out. Fire fighting is left to the trained experts.

The security of a system depends not only upon one's own people and their care, honesty and integrity. Often outside agencies are essential for all kinds of utility services, like electricity, water and sewage disposal. Firms usually use contract maintenance engineering services on the computer itself, and on things like air-conditioning plants and fire protection systems. Industrial relations problems can pose real difficulties. The problem may be insurmountable if a vital service or supply is affected in this way, and no alternative is available. It is hard to deal with any kind of industrial action. It is especially difficult if the problem lies within control of another organisation.

Personnel policy is therefore a vital consideration in any security programme.

Staffing and personnel policies in a computer department will necessarily form part of a wider corporate personnel policy. Much can be done in selection and recruitment to improve security standards by reducing risks. Many potential problems involving employees can be avoided if the recruitment policies of an organisation are well planned and adhered to. It is just as important for security that recruits find job satisfaction and feel justly paid, as it is to ensure that their references and background are acceptable to the organisation. Once recruited, it is essential to monitor the well-being of employees. Proper training and staff development policies, if honestly pursued, may reduce the likelihood of grievances and employee unrest. This will minimise the chances of bad relations interfering with the system.

If it should be necessary to terminate the employment of an individual this should be carried out through established company procedures. Staff termination procedures are frequently lax, leaving loopholes in the corporate security measures. Once the action to dismiss has been agreed, steps should be taken to ensure that the employee has no opportunity to perform any breach of security. He should be removed from sensitive areas of work and required to give up his identification badges, cards and keys.

Recruitment should be done by a personnel officer professionally trained for the work, and with experience of data processing staff. Where high levels of security are essential it may be desirable to advertise vacancies under a box number. It then becomes much harder for another organisation to plant somebody. All applicants for employment in computer areas should be screened, and vetted, according to the needs of the particular post. Normal selection procedures can establish the suitability of applicants in technical and personality aspects. It is much more difficult to establish an applicant's suitability for the organisation, to discover potential problems, such as those due to drink, drug-taking, gambling, previous criminal convictions or acts at previous places of employment which may never have been taken to court. These acts may include dishonesty, vandalism, damage amounting to sabotage, and industrial disruption arising from political beliefs. Care must be taken regarding possible previous criminal convictions, as it is in general no longer legitimate, as a consequence of the Rehabilitation of Offenders Act 1974, to question applicants about this.

Successful personal vetting of applicants requires that the prospective employer has carefully defined the level of security necessary for the post, taking into account the existing security policies and procedures. Confidential enquiries concerning the applicant should be carried out by the personnel officer or by the manager of the department with the vacancy. Personal interview or telephone discussion is usually more effective than asking for written references. Where government defence contracts are involved, assistance may be given with vetting enquiries. Details are given in the appropriate government manual supplied to the organisation. Some private security organisations specialise in this type of work. The police in the United Kingdom will give no information about previous convictions.

Inevitably some people will leave their employment. They may do so to further their career or they may retire. Sometimes they may be dismissed by the employer. Whatever the cause, terminating employment offers opportunities for breaches of security to occur. Different circumstances determine the extent of these potential breaches. The events and procedures leading to a dismissal often adversely affect the morale, and hence the security, of an organisation.

Employees who give notice of resignation should be removed from security-sensitive activities as soon as possible and preferably at once. In the case of a key employee dealing with sensitive information and giving notice, it is necessary for management, colleagues and his outside business contacts to be informed immediately.

Firms often lose assets when an employee leaves. Keys and identification badges should be returned. All documentation and manuals ought to be accounted for, together with library books and other borrowed materials. Tools and equipment are sometimes overlooked. Company credit-cards and items of business stationery should be surrendered.

Passwords, identifications and entries in authorisation tables should be cancelled. Arrangements should be made to pass to the employee's replacement ownership of files, data, programs and documentation. Someone will need to be assigned tasks that were in progress. The employee's name and his workstation should be removed from the computer- and manually-generated distribution lists.

On termination, employees should be required to reaffirm their undertaking to observe the confidentiality of the information to which they have had access. An employee should be reminded of any restrictions that exist in working in competition for whatever period of time.

Whenever possible, essential duties should be delegated to other staff on a temporary basis (with financial rewards, if these are appropriate). Top priority should be given to the process of recruiting a replacement. The administrative procedures all too often inhibit and delay the recruitment process. Management waits until the departure of an employee before even initiating the recruitment of the replacement.

Relationships with outside organisations will suffer in the period between departure and replacement if proper arrangements have not been made. This may have long-term effects on the business. Customers may be lost to competitors, for example.

Deviations from normal working methods rendered necessary during this period may also tend to weaken security. Personnel might more easily be able to carry out unauthorised duties without arousing suspicion.

Termination of employment from whatever cause is a normal occurrence within an organisation. Managements should therefore have adequate plans formulated to handle it and its implications for security.

ORGANISATION ASPECTS

It must not be assumed that people are trustworthy. As few people as possible should be entrusted with matters involving security. Research in the United States indicates that only one person in four is inherently honest. That implies that three people out of four are not to be trusted. The figures elsewhere and in other organisations may be different.

Nevertheless, employees pose threats for security. The threats may come from inexperience and lack of training. Incompetence and negligence are not unusual. Deliberate threats of fraud, arson and malicious damage should be borne in mind. Job organisation offers one way of improving security.

The need to know principle is useful. Information given to employees should be limited to that which is needed to do their job. Information about the whole system should not be freely available. Employees engaged on order entry do not need to know how new accounts are established, and, still less, how the payroll is run. The principle applies generally, not just to sensitive information. Care will obviously be taken to safeguard information like passwords and identifiers. If possible, knowledge about the administrative controls and procedures should be limited to those with a need to know.

Systems analysts are often in a very privileged position. As a necessary part of their duties they obtain overall, yet detailed, information on company systems. Their knowledge about these systems is often far more detailed and thorough than that of the people who actually operate and use them. This knowledge tends to cross functional boundaries between the different parts of an organisation. It thus circumvents the classical controls by segregation of duties. Care should be taken, therefore, to ensure that systems analysts do not have operational access to systems.

Other job functions should be arranged so as to minimise, and where possible avoid, unnecessary interaction between personnel performing different jobs. Systems programmers should only be allowed in the computer room when this is essential. Ordinary staff programmers should have no privileges beyond those of normal users, except, possibly access to special terminals.

Staff members should be fully aware of job and authority limitations. They should also know the consequences of exceeding this authority. Access control systems should be arranged to ensure that the authorised access rules are maintained. No unauthorised person should be admitted to the computer room, data preparation or control areas, to the tape library or other restricted zones. If it should be necessary for a normally unauthorised person to enter such an area, they should be accompanied at all times by an authorised person.

Another important principle is avoidance of sole control. One individual should not be left in control of important operations. This is particularly true for computer operators where a sole operator in complete control would constitute a security risk. At least one other operator should be present both for security and safety reasons. Temporary or newly recruited staff, and staff under training should not be trusted with sole charge of security sensitive operations.

If possible, systems should be so designed that input and output documents reveal as little as possible to computer room staff. Such documents should be seen and handled by as few people as possible. Data preparation staff do not need to know the purpose of the data that they punch. They do not need to know the user's name or even his department. Labelling of disks and tapes need not indicate their real usage. All waste should be destroyed as soon as possible.

Another important principle that can be used in organisations is that of split authority. The idea is that the authority to carry out some important activity is split between two people. Two separate keys are needed to access the strong room, for example. A very common instance is the requirement for two signatures on a cheque, selected perhaps from three authorised signatories.

This principle can be extended in many ways. It is not necessary to have two physical keys. Administrative procedures can employ the idea to gain increased security. Where sensitive processing is carried out, a designated person might be included within the administrative procedure. This is quite often done with payroll, or cheque printing runs on computer systems. Another way of handling sensitive payroll, incidentally, is to run it on a bureau elsewhere.

Changes to passwords and new user identifiers are particularly sensitive issues. Control of these might be vested in a manager and carried out by a specified individual. In this way the manager would not be able to change the password without cooperation from the other party. Furthermore the programmer would have no authority to make such changes without the manager's prior written authority. In modern systems password control is often done automatically within the computer system itself.

Complete segregation of duties and application of the need to know principle may cause problems for small installations. For one thing the number of staff in such an installation may be so small that realistic segregation is impossible in anything but name. Moreover, such isolation of duties introduces another danger. There is a lack of job cover for absences. Clearly an organisation has to provide and train some other person to cover holidays and other absences. This is vital for all essential functions.

There is also a real danger that someone may become the 'complete expert' in a key area. No-one else available would be able to cope, especially if the documentation is inadequate. A useful test is to consider whether a competent person from elsewhere in the organisation could handle the job without a period of handover from the normal encumbant. If not, there is a threat to the system. Such a situation should be avoided by ensuring that a trained understudy is available for each important function.

All employees should receive adequate instructions about how to handle dangerous situations. These include fire, bomb threats, flood, armed entry and structural failure. The response required will differ in each case. Unless they have been well briefed, staff may be unable to handle the problems properly. It is up to management to plan in advance and formulate adequate instructions. Proper training will be needed for key staff.

Finally we should consider the position of personnel in a contingency situation, following a disaster. The first point to bear in mind is that the usual staff may not be available. In the UK we are very fortunate. Natural disasters affecting computers are usually small in scale, and personal injury and death are uncommon. In some other countries this is not the case. Nature can be very violent. Also, fire and terrorist attacks are far more significant threats elsewhere in Europe.

The contingency plans formulated by the organisation will take this into account. The plans will be established with first and second alternates for each functional role. This is standard practice. The people so designated in the contingency plan must be properly trained. They should be briefed about their role and if possible should work through it in advance of a real disaster.

One might have to ask staff to work under trying conditions after a disaster. Perhaps they may be away from home, with a bad journey to and from the back-up site. Some staff will not tolerate these conditions for long, unless morale is very high. Everything possible should be done to minimise the problems faced by staff. The costs involved form part of the total cost of the contingency. The staff will be working longer hours than usual. They will be under extra pressure to complete the work. The equipment and conditions may be unfamiliar. The work pattern required will differ from normal. In fact, planning for people in a disaster is one of the hardest problems in the whole security field. There are no ideal solutions. Any realistic plans are likely to be better than none at all.

6 Hardware

One of the most significant points about computers from a security viewpoint is often overlooked. Computers can be arranged to check their operations themselves. The hardware today includes all kinds of checks in an attempt to detect errors, and sometimes even to correct them. The user is often unaware of just how extensive this checking has become on modern equipment. It is so effective that it can be ignored by the user.

An important factor leading to this development has been the declining cost of hardware. It is now feasible to devote very significant portions of the hardware to checking the working of the systems. Moreover, the systems are now so complex and big, that built-in checking is almost essential if the system is to function at all reliably.

Modern processors include special engineering controls. They will detect malfunctions and record the details so that the engineer can examine the records at a later date. There may be facilities so that the engineer can test portions of the equipment while the rest of it is in normal service. The cost may be a slight reduction in the processing throughput. There will nearly always be special diagnostic facilities to help the engineer find faulty components and units. Some manufacturers have used remote testing to speed up the process. The suspect machine is hooked-up via a telephone circuit to a remote diagnostic testing centre. This exercises the local machine, and finds out what is wrong with it. The special machine can do this much more consistently and more quickly than can the local site engineer.

Modern hardware is very much more reliable and trouble-free than earlier equipment. Faults are rare. Engineers, as a consequence, have little experience of finding faults. The equipment tends to be more complex, and any faults that do occur are possibly more difficult to find unless the very best techniques are used. The user has come to demand higher availability, so that only very minimum downtime is acceptable. The pressure for good engineering service is therefore very great.

Units like disks and tape transports include checks to ensure that data is not in error. The usual techniques include parity checks on blocks of data. The bits representing a character include an extra parity bit, which is arranged to be zero or one so as to make the total number of one bits in the representation either even (for 'even-parity'), or, less commonly, odd (for 'odd-parity').

The hardware can detect parity failure on individual characters, usually because one bit is in error. Blocks of parity-protected characters are checked by block sum checks of various kinds. One common method is the Cyclic Redundancy Check (CRC). It uses a complex algorithm to calculate a special check sum which is written at the end of the block. Logic can check the data, and compare the calculated sum with the stored check once again. Discrepancies can point up the sort of error that has occurred. This kind of check is used on magnetic media and in communication links. Minor errors can often be corrected by the hardware.

On disks the data is stored in blocks. Sometimes a particular block on the disk contains a permanent flaw, so that data cannot be recorded properly. At first sight, such a failure would render the expensive disk pack quite useless. However, the disk system contains a map showing which blocks are flawed, and indicating for each one which reserve block should be used instead. The substitution takes place automatically when the disk is used without anyone being aware of it. In fact one needs to run a special engineers program to discover whether any flaws exist on a cartridge pack.

These are examples of the kinds of hardware checks that are included by the manufacturer as part of the equipment design. The user has no control, except by selecting a different manufacturer/ model.

Some kinds of hardware malfunction are properly the concern of the user. The most important are probably media and printer error controls. Most modern systems will check magnetic tape transports during use, and record all failures in some sort of engineering or systems file. These records should be analysed as a routine matter. The analysis will draw attention to recurrent failure of particular media. It will separate media faults from tape transport faults. Media and transport faults are of low incidence in well conducted centres. The problem is how to minimise the remaining incidents. Usually it is best to enrol the machine itself as an ally, and use it to process the available data.

Printers can print wrong characters, even given the correct data. Often the mistake is obvious, as in the mis-spelling of a word, but sometimes it may be concealed. The most difficult case is when an odd decimal digit is wrongly printed. It may well be accepted, leading to wrong decisions.

Various checks are possible. The first aim ought to be to give visibility to the problem. End users should be encouraged to report any poor or faulty printing, no matter how benign the effect. If printing errors exist in one job they may exist elsewhere in less obvious places. Engineering support can be alerted.

It is possible to run test data through the printer in repetitive, but random patterns, so that the odd 'wrong' character can be spotted. Such output is often called 'wallpaper'. The installation can produce its own test programs and run them every day to give some confidence. Ordinary application programs are likely to be a more effective test than typical engineer tests. Printer faults are often time-dependent. The engineer has a vested interest in proving that the printer is good. The security man wants to find even a rare intermittent defect before it spoils real output.

Obviously all critical output ought to be designed on the basis that the figures may be wrongly printed. Cheque protection using words and figures is a sensible measure. Vital figures can be cross totalled, and manually checked at data control.

One other aspect of hardware security is worth consideration. This is the existence of residual data in various places, which may give rise to breach of confidentiality.

Suppose that a magnetic tape is used to hold output data from some intermediate stage in say a payroll run. The tape is read by another program in the suite. It is then scratched, and made available for further use. At this stage it will usually contain the data from the payroll run. The physical and magnetic header labels may have changed. The data down the tape will still exist, however. In principle another program could be used to read it, especially in engineers' mode, thus revealing the data to unauthorised eyes. There are two solutions to this problem. One is to delete the data either by writing over it by program before releasing the media, or by using a special degausser, which erases the magnetic image. The other solution is to retain the reel of tape within control of the (payroll) system, and not allow it to be used for other purposes. The problem of residues on magnetic tape is taken seriously by many organisations. Some do not even trust degaussing for very sensitive data. In case of damage to disks or tapes, they insist that the media are destroyed by physical disintegration. Great care should be taken with any media exchanged with other sites. Incoming media should be checked, possibly cleaned, before use. Any outgoing media should be controlled to ensure that they contain no data except what was intended, and that they go only to the correct recipient.

The performance and fault history of the equipment and its individual units should be monitored in cooperation with the maintenance engineers. Records of availability should be kept, so that changes can be investigated.

7 Software

Computer software includes both applications programs and systems software. Application programs normally include controls to ensure that the correct processing is done on the correct files. There will be checks from run to run, to be certain that the right numbers of records are handled, and so on. Many error detection techniques will be used to guard against accidents and deliberate dishonesty.

All applications software rests upon a foundation of systems software, usually provided by the manufacturer of the particular machine. This includes the language system, such as a COBOL compiler, with various utility programs and standard subroutine libraries. Most important of all from the security viewpoint is the operating system, which controls and monitors the entire workload of the installation.

Many cases of computer abuse and malpractice could have been prevented if systems software had been designed with adequate security protection features. Several developments within the last few years have heightened the need for good security features in software, and exposed the weaknesses of many existing products.

Traditional batch processing incorporated several levels of protection. Data processing jobs had to be submitted through a job control office before they could be run on the machine. All input and output to the system was subject to scrutiny, and any unusual output would be visible to control staff. Moreover all work was logged, and the turn-round time was relatively long, so that an attempted fraud or unauthorised operation was visible, and a quick 'kill' was hard to achieve.

These batch systems have been overtaken by multi-user systems providing immediate access to data and to powerful processing facilities. The work being done on terminals is often 'invisible' to operations staff in the DP department.

Terminals are located in user departments, frequently on remote sites with poor or non-existent access controls. They may even be mobile, on dial-up telephone connections. Control of access to processing, and its separation from data control provided a significant barrier in the traditional batch environment. Its effect on efficiency was one reason for widescale provision of on-line terminal systems, available to user staff.

A significant feature of modern systems is their extreme flexibility. A user at a terminal can switch quickly from one application to another, and can move from data entry to interrogation, from program development to report production. Data processing department staff may have little or no information about what the users are doing and what work is being done on the system at any point in time.

Users are concerned about their data, about who can access it, and more importantly about who is able to change it. The fact that users think of data as belonging to them is significant. Data processing departments are in reality custodians of a user department's data. Somehow they must protect that data to the satisfaction of the user department. In the batch days one could do this to some extent by good media controls and an adequate librarian function, but this is no longer possible. Moreover, users do want to allow other departments to have controlled access to some of their data, say to particular fields but not to others. They may allow these other users to read the data or to change it, so that different kinds of data access control are needed. There may be a requirement to hide the fact of data existence from unauthorised view, a fact that has significance in design of system error reports as we shall see.

The other major factor is that more and more business operations have migrated towards computer systems. There has been a massive shift from clerical systems towards computer systems. The systems are not simply a replacement for the clerical paperwork systems. In many cases the computer systems effect transfer of assets, either in money or by producing goods movement instructions. For example, early DP systems printed cheques, which were then subjected to manual scrutiny. Modern systems must interface directly with the banking system. Volumes have increased to such an extent that they commonly generate despatch notes and later keep the sales invoices and accounting details, almost entirely on the basis of internal transactions. Without proper controls there are clearly many opportunities for things to go wrong, either by accident or intentionally.

It is worth noting also that the traditional 'people' controls tend to be lost as computer systems are extended in scope and complexity. For instance the segregation of authorisation of a new credit customer from the acceptance of sales orders may be lost in that both kinds of transaction may be available to many staff in on-line systems.

Systems are also subject to attack by another group whose motive is not personal gain. There are small numbers of people intent on destroying the credibility of computer systems, vandals if you like, who simply want to cause the maximum amount of difficulty and embarrassment for users and managements.

The possible legal implications of poor software controls must be considered. Evidence from computer systems will be input in cases of fraud or other computer abuse. If this evidence is to be acceptable it is usually necessary to show, for example, that the system was well-conducted, and that the evidence could not have been generated in error.

SECURITY SOFTWARE FEATURES

The base software of an installation, the operating system, ought to include a set of security features to provide automatic protection. In principle the security features can be provided by the manufacturer as part of the operating system, or they can be added to the basic operating system as a security package. Both approaches are in vogue.

The advantage of building security features into the operating system itself is that it is much harder to evade them, especially for systems staff. It they are part of the system it is very difficult to strip them away. On the other hand, because they form part of the operating software their nature is that much more exposed to systems programmers, who may be able to devise ways of defeating the controls.

An add-on security package is the exact opposite. It is inherently possible to run the operating system without the package, which may be important in back-up situations on an alien site. It is possible to run without the security package on one's own site also, without authority perhaps. A package can be a closed-book so far as most staff are concerned, so that the way it works and the features it provides by way of monitoring need be known only to internal audit staff, for example.

The software system must do three things:

— identify each and every system user;

— maintain access controls over data, programs, processes and resources, so that only authorised users are allowed to access them in permitted ways;

— maintain a log of all usage for subsequent analysis by audit personnel, and alert appropriate staff in case of any attempted breach of the security rules.

Clearly the systems controls must themselves be secure. It should not be possible to evade the checks or to corrupt the audit log.

The cost of adequate security features may be very high in both terms of development and in terms of overhead in normal system operation. As usual some balance needs to be struck. In early attempts to develop secure systems enormous resources were devoted to the projects. Many studies of penetration of operating systems are recorded. It is usually fairly easy for skilled software engineers to breach the defences of an operating system. The published user documentation often gives a great deal of help in devising ways of evading checks. The usual problem is not to breach the defences, but to discover some information that is useful among the vast amounts of data held in typical systems.

The appropriate measure for the level of system protection is how much it would cost the hostile agent to access the system successfully as against his potential gain. Providing great protection at one point may only drive the hostile agent to attack another point that is less well protected. Therefore the security measures should be balanced with no gaps in the defences. Software controls must form part of the security measures.

Adequate software protection is hard to achieve because in principle any program that runs on a processor can access any information available to the processor. Such a program can retrieve, alter or destroy information at the will of the programmer. What one programmer puts together another can take apart.

Early attempts at creating secure operating systems concentrated attention on patching over the gaps or holes, in effect repairing the potential breaches. The trouble with this is that the process is never complete. Even when every known hole that allows a penetration approach is repaired, there must still be other avenues open to the potential attacker. A minor but important practical point is that repairing the holes in a system may mean that existing legitimate programs and applications no longer work. Another problem with the patching holes approach is that the complex and expensive program modifications that may be needed in the operating system may well introduce further holes into the fabric, in what were previously sound areas. This has analogies in ordinary applications programming, where successive layers of modification and enhancement, introduced to meet changed user requirements, may gradually render the entire structure unsound.

Inherently Secure Systems

Much work has been devoted to the design of inherently secure operating systems. The kernel approach was developed in the 1970s. A security kernel is a hardware and software implementation of a concept that enforces formal security rules in a computer system. It controls access of active system elements like users, programs and processes to objects like information, registers, programs and terminals. The implementation of the kernel is relatively simple, and can be separated from the implementation of the large complex operating system. The security mechanism is isolated from the rest of the operating system.

The kernel must be:

- complete, in that it must be invoked on every attempt to access objects;

- isolated in that it cannot be changed or evaded;

- verified, in that it must operate correctly under all circumstances.

The kernel approach has drawbacks. It can lead to an inflexible system because of the difficulty of separating the security rules from the mechanism that enforces them. However, stability of the rules is an important aid to secure systems. A kernel may also constitute a bottleneck in the system, since every access to objects in the system must invoke it. It is possible that the kernel approach could be implemented partly in hardware, which might increase both the efficiency and certainty of the technique.

Another approach is to design a new system that can be shown to be secure. SRI International developed a hardware-independent design for the PSOS (provably secure operating system). Among the design aims were that the system should:

- enforce multi-level security properties that were mathematically provable;

- be realisable and have an efficient implementation;

- not be constrained by existing hardware;

- provide a flexible system base that can be extended to fit a variety of user needs.

Development of secure operating systems will be costly. Potential users, which means most of us, should compare the likely costs with the potential business losses from exposure if their system remains insecure.

Major manufacturers need to be convinced of the commercial feasibility of developing and marketing secure operating systems. Today such systems are not available, and there is a ready market for packages that go some way towards the aim of making systems secure.

A Typical Operating System – GEORGE 3

GEORGE 3 is an operating system for the major ICL 1900 and

2900 computers. It is a large system, developed over a decade on varied hardware, and with the benefit of a huge exposure to real commercial work.

In GEORGE 3 one of the fundamentals is the filestore concept, in which resources are allocated on a descending tree. Users have a place in this hierarchy represented by a directory file, somewhere on the tree. The directory holds details about all the files, programs, tapes and other objects owned by the user.

Only users who are known to the system, and who have a place in the tree can run any work or access the system, except in very primitive modes. Each user has a username of up to 12 alphanumerics, which is used in job control and other communications with the system. Users also have a password, again up to 12 characters, which they must use in order to log in on a terminal.

GEORGE 3 has a system of access control traps which apply to every object in the filestore. Normally the user is allowed to access his own objects in any of the permitted modes. These are READ, WRITE, APPEND (that is add to the end of a file, but not overwrite existing data), EXECUTE (to permit execution of a program or a program-like object) and ERASE (which allows the object to be destroyed by the user).

The user can stop any of these modes of access by issue of a TRAPSTOP command on the object. For example, he can prevent himself from accidentally destroying a program by a command like

TRAPSTOP MYPROG, ERASE

and he can reverse this later by a TRAPGO command

TRAPGO MYPROG, ERASE.

He can also give permission to the operating system to let other people access his objects using the TRAPGO command, but he must do this separately for each object. For instance, he can allow FRED access to MYFILE in READ mode by the command

TRAPGO MYFILE, : FRED READ

and he can also do this for a whole branch of the filestore tree using the GROUP concept of FRED and all his inferiors on the tree, eg

TRAPGO MYFILE, : FRED, GROUP, READ

would allow FRED and all his inferiors to read MYFILE. The username MANAGER represents a user at the head of the tree and superior to all the actual users. Access can be allowed to all users by the command

TRAPGO MYFILE, : MANAGER, GROUP, READ.

The trapping concept is very powerful, but hard to manage efficiently. For one thing the traps that apply to an object do not get carried forward to successor generations of the object. They have to be specifically applied by job control statements.

In consequence users tend to open traps and leave them open, because it is troublesome to go round and stop them again. Another defect of the trapping system in GEORGE is that it can provide information to an attacker. There is a TRAPCHECK command that enables the user to discover the state of the access traps (so far as he is concerned) on any object in the filestore. If he is permitted access to the object the reply tells him what modes are allowed. On the other hand if he is denied access the reply still allows him to check for the existence of the object, since if it exists the reply is to the effect that he has no permitted modes of access, whereas if he trapchecks a non-existent object he gets a command error. This is typical of the kind of minor security hole that exists in good modern operating systems.

GEORGE 3 has a powerful system journal facility that logs all significant events. This could be used to provide an audit trail for security violation, and attempted breaches. The journal system can be invoked by file access mechanisms, and it is totally invisible to ordinary users. Close supervision of the system journal, and regular analysis of it by audit staff could provide a powerful control feature.

GEORGE 3 has a password mechanism that applies mainly to terminal users who wish to log in to the system. There are several defects in the system. The password is associated not with an external person, but with a collection of objects in the filestore. It is very common for several people to need to work on the same filestore objects as part of a particular project. GEORGE 3 treats the group as a single user, so that several individuals must share the same password.

In practice most passwords are short, because the user can set his own password, and people try to save effort. Within GEORGE 3 there is a mechanism for creating a pseudo terminal job, as a program running under control of another program. One user constructed a pseudo job of this kind which was able to explore all possible passwords up to 6 or 7 characters in but a few seconds. Given a user name it was quite simple to let the program discover the corresponding password. The pseudo terminal job could be invoked, do its job and be deleted long before the system monitor system reported the first violation to the system operators, because of the 'long' delays in message processing.

GEORGE 3 has relatively good protection mechanisms to prevent users from gaining unauthorised access to data and programs that belong to other users. It does have an extensive repertoire of commands for the systems programmer who can have virtually unlimited access to anything in the system. There is a system of privileges that can be given to or withdrawn from users by the system manager. Possession of a privilege allows a user to do certain things; without the appropriate privilege the user cannot do the privileged operation. For instance, the user might be given a privilege that allows him to read the system journal. Another privilege might allow him to append information of specified kinds into the journal. (He would not be able to simulate messages put in the journal by other parts of the operating system.)

GEORGE 3 also has a comprehensive LIBRARIAN mechanism that looks after magnetic tapes in dynamic fashion. Tapes are known to the system librarian by tape serial number which is assumed to be invariant, since it can only be changed under control of the librarian. Most tapes are owned by users in the filestore, and have access traps in the same way as other objects. No other user can access a tape without permission of the owner. There is no way in which the user can evade the librarian without special cooperation from the console operating staff. This may be necessary to handle data interchange from other sites, or for other legitimate purposes. Because it is dynamic – it is invoked as soon as a tape is mounted – the librarian provides one of the most effective protections against accidental errors in tape usage, and this contributes to the security of the installation.

Security Packages

There are several security packages that are added to the standard IBM operating systems to give more protection. The best known are SECURE, RACF (Resource Access Control Facility) and ACF2 (Access Control Facility), all of which can be used in conjunction with System 370 operating system OS/VS2 (MVS).

These packages provide control over access to the system, so that all users are positively identified. They then control access to data sets and to other system resources. All the packages complement the standard operating system by exploiting hooks or by replacement of standard routines. They all record logging information in the system monitor file SMF, so that accesses can be analysed for audit purposes. Usually there is provision for analysing the logging information with special audit utilities. The packages implement the kinds of control over access and usage that are an essential part of any supposedly secure environment. They vary in their techniques.

SECURE

SECURE is a data access security system developed and maintained by Boole and Babbage Inc of Sunnyvale, California. It is a replacement for the standard IBM password facility of OS, VS or MVS operating systems. The replacement modules automatically assemble an Access Identifier String (AIS) of 64 bytes from important fields in the job's JCL using one of a set of user specified algorithms. This AIS can be considered as an abbreviation of the JCL. SECURE retrieves the AIS from a security file, and determines the validity of the access from parameters recorded in the security file with AIS. Thus the access that is allowed relates to the particular job and user. The fact that a user can submit a job with legal access to a particular data set does not imply that he is allowed access to this same data set on other jobs, or even on another set up of this same job.

SECURE does not provide additional password protection over the access that a TSO user has to the computing system, but it may require the user to provide one to access protected data sets.

Access can be controlled at several levels – execute only, read only, update only (no rename or scratch), control internal (VSAM) and master.

SECURE includes a collection of utilities for operations like security file backup, cross reference listing of the security file, repair of damaged or corrupted files.

SECURE is implemented by using hooks in OS password protection, in which existing routines are replaced by new routines. Certain audit routines are provided as part of the package in a multipurpose audit package. This can produce reports about the different kinds of access attempts, at levels of detail selected by the user. All logging is done to SMF, and unsuccessful access attempts are always logged and reported also to the security console, and to the master system operator if desired. Separate reports can be produced for users and for auditors.

The overhead with SECURE is very low indeed. In one large benchmark test there was no measurable effect on throughput, and a 0.01% increase in CPU.

RACF

Resource Access Control Facility, RACF, is the IBM product to support System/370 OS/VS2(MVS). It gives access control by identifying and verifying system users, authorising access to direct access storage devices, data sets, and by logging accesses to protected data sets and unauthorised attempts at system access.

Access is controlled by user knowledge of a password, which is controlled and may be changed by the user. The password is 1 to 8 alphanumeric characters. It can be supplemented or replaced by an operator identification card. RACF provides audit facilities, and writes records to SMF. It also constructs statistical profiles.

ACF2

ACF2 is supplied by the Cambridge Systems Group, Los Altos Hills, California. It is a supplementary package for IBM operating system MVS. It provides control of access to the system using passwords and logonids, and control of access to data on direct access and tape storage devices.

ACF2 protects all data by default instead of needing explicit protection statements.

A user is identified by an 8-character log-on identifier and an associated password. The length of the password is variable, and the installation may set a minimum acceptable length and a password change interval. ACF2 maintains a database to control access, and there are seven sections of ACF2 information in the logonid record.

The first section, Identification Section, contains the user's logonid, name, password, telephone number and UID (User Identification String). The access rules, which control access to data sets (ie data files), and the resource rules, which control access to logical resources (eg types of transaction, account numbers), contain an optional UID field (if this is omitted, all user identification strings will match by default), which if present specifies the user identification strings to which a rule applies. The UID in the Identification Section has a maximum length of 24 characters and a default value of the logonid. This string may include, in addition to the logonid, characters representing user division, user department, job responsibility within department, employee identification number, etc.

The second section, Cancel/Suspend section, shows whether a logonid has been cancelled or suspended, and if so when and by whom (eg by a security officer). Suspension may occur because a logonid has been accompanied by an incorrect password more frequently than an installation standard permits. This section also shows whether a logonid is being traced or monitored; for example, an auditor may want to do this.

The third section, Privileges Section, shows whether a user is permitted to do certain things. For example, 'account' indicates the ability to insert, delete and modify logonid records; 'consult' indicates the ability to display other logonid records; 'leader' indicates the ability to display and alter certain fields of members of a project; and 'security' indicates that the user is a security officer who is able to create and inspect access rules, and set certain fields in logonid records. These privileges may be granted on a total system basis or limited by using the 'dsnscope' mask (to limit the scope of a security officer when applied to data set references), the 'lidscope' mask (to limit the scope of an authorised user when applied to logonid records), or the 'uidscope' mask (to determine which logonid records may be modified by an authorised user). The 'restrict' field indicates that the logonid may be used without password verification, but jobs submitted with a logonid which is restricted will be journalled and displayed on a special report (the Restricted Logonid Job Log report).

The fourth section, Access Section, records the number of system accesses, and the date and time of the last system access by the logonid.

The fifth section, Miscellaneous Section, includes 'maxdays' – this is the maximum number of days allowed between password changes, (zero indicates no limit).

The sixth section, TSO Section, is provided for use when UADS (User Attribute Data Set of TSO) is by-passed. It contains the fields which are normally found in that data set.

The seventh and final section, Statistics Section, has information about password and security violations for the logonid, and the date and time when the password and the logonid record were last updated.

ACF2 includes a fairly powerful set of audit facilities. The Security Officer can ask ACF2 to monitor usage by a particular user. This allows realtime monitoring on the security console and detailed subsequent reporting. Logging is done to SMF (System Monitor File).

ACF2 inserts 'hooks' into the MVS supervisor to gain control during new data set allocation, open, rename, scratch and catalogue processing. ACF2 then determines whether access should be allowed automatically or whether further verification is needed.

Not only does ACF2 control access to data sets, but it also protects logical resources, such as transactions, account numbers or procedure names.

Access control rules in ACF2 are grouped and compiled into a set of rule object records. Data set names may be grouped under one access rule, by combinations of groups of character strings each representing one data set name. Within each character string, masking can be achieved by using asterisks to represent any character including blank.

The overhead involved in using ACF2 is minimal. The CPU time is less than 1% with 100% of data protected.

CONCLUSION

At present, manufacturers' operating systems are not sufficiently secure for today's needs. The kinds of facility provided by the access control packages that have become available in the last few years mark a distinct improvement in the level of control that can be achieved. Control is needed over access to data, programs and other physical objects.

The less obvious point is that control over access to different kinds of processing resources is equally vital. For instance, suppose that X is not allowed to access object Y. Can he access the mechanism that allows him to change this state of affairs? If not, is there any way in which he can change the arrangements at the next level? Logically, the protection may exist within the system. The importance of good logging is that changes of this sort should be logged in a system journal or monitor file that is itself protected from corruption. Changes in the access permissions for sensitive data may then be examined by the security auditor.

The importance of constant vigilance cannot be over-emphasised. It is too easy to believe that one's security measures are adequate, and that no holes exist. In any good system, all significant events should be monitored and recorded automatically without the knowledge of the ordinary user or the systems and operations staff. These records should be analysed routinely to pinpoint any abnormal activity. Such continuing systems audit may well reveal deficiencies in the software or in the operations procedures.

8 Computer Fraud and Other Misuse

example of fraud

A 25-year-old computer terminal operator in an insurance company managed to secure for herself payments of pensions under 30 different names, making herself a comfortable income. Her scheme was a simple one. When pensioners died it was her job to enter the details at her keyboard. She had discovered that she could enter change of address instructions instead, so she did this from time to time. By using an accomplice's address the flow of monthly cheques was thus augmented yet again. When the auditors wrote and asked for confirmation that the pensioner was still alive – as they do from time to time – they naturally received confirmation by return. She was eventually caught because the controls were better than she realised, though not really adequate to prevent the original abuse.

Computer fraud is not yet a serious problem in the UK – in contrast to the situation in the United States. In 1980 the losses from fraud and other abuse of computer systems there were estimated to exceed $300 million.

There are two conflicting views about fraud in general and computer fraud in particular. Facts are sparse. One view is that there are very few cases and that the problem is microscopic. Few cases are reported, it is true. The opposing view is that this is because there is no incentive for organisations to report computer fraud. What we see according to this view is therefore merely the tip of the iceberg, and, it is suggested, there exists a huge body of undeclared and indeed undiscovered fraud. What is the reality?

A survey in 1981 by the Local Government Audit Inspectorate

69

received 319 replies, with 67 cases of computer related crime over the previous five years. The total reported loss was under £1M, and the largest single loss was £230,000 over 2 years from a duplicate payments fraud. The replies to the survey were treated in strict confidence. Even so, very few cases were brought to light. The results of this survey may be misleading.

Ordinary commercial fraud is very common. The police report well over 100,000 cases each year, and are probably aware of many times this number of suspected cases. Criminal statistics are not to be relied upon, and the police record only a fraction of reported cases.

One might therefore be tempted to dismiss computer fraud and other abuse as a problem of no importance. It is likely that the figures will grow simply because of the migration of business systems into computers. Crime tends to follow opportunity. If the opportunities exist in computer systems the criminals will find them. This has already happened in North America where the penetration of computing is so much greater than in Europe.

Not all computer frauds are trivial. The case of Equity Funding Life Insurance Company in Los Angeles, California is a case that has been widely discussed. Officers and employees set up some 63,000 bogus insurance policies in three years, worth some $1600 million. They sold these bogus policies to other insurance companies in the reinsurance business. Given wide television coverage as 'The Billion Dollar Bubble', the fraud involved mass collusion, including a computer programmer. The programmer produced the suite of programs needed to create the bogus policies, pay commissions, create fake reports, maintain balances, and interface with the genuine business.

The case was significant by virtue of its size. The computer was incidental to the main fraud. It was needed simply to process the huge amount of false transactions and paperwork.

Another significant early case occurred at the Union Dime Savings Bank. A chief teller embezzled $1.5 million by transferring money from legitimate accounts to fraudulent ones, and then withdrawing the money. He was able to make accounts appear in balance by shuffling amounts between accounts with very large balances. A very high staff turnover in the department allowed him to explain inconsistencies as being clerical errors. The system was completely on-line. This did not make the theft easier, but it did make it faster.

Most reported cases are much smaller and less spectacular. Steady growth has been recorded in the United States, where several hundred cases have been analysed.

There are unconfirmed reports of a recent smash-and-grab case on the international electronic fund transfer system. This involved reprogramming a machine so that it could be activated on a selected day. The program then watched for large incoming transfers. It created duplicate outgoing transfers to a Swiss account, and never recorded the incoming transactions. Within a short space, a huge amount had been diverted.

In a case in Devon in 1978 a former bank manager was convicted of defrauding his employers of £737. His scheme depended on the bank's method of handling spoilt cheques. In the clearing system these are segregated and sent to the drawer's branch for attention. The manager spoiled cheques drawn on his own account to pay shops and tradesmen. The cheques were met by the bank, but were rejected by the central bureau and sent back for attention. The manager simply destroyed them so that his account was never debited. The bank had good controls, so he was eventually caught.

One of the largest hauls reported from one incident in the UK was in 1977 when the cargo system at Heathrow Airport was apparently reprogrammed to divert a consignment so that it by-passed customs examination. Some £2 million of cannabis from Uganda was thus imported illegally. This is an illustration of the fact that cash is not a necessary ingredient for a successful coup. Almost any kind of goods or services are saleable somewhere. You do not have to have access to financial systems.

The Penn Central Railroad had a computer system to control the routeing of freight cars. It was discovered that 217 large box cars were missing, and investigation showed that the programs had been modified to route them to a small railroad system. Here they were discovered, freshly painted in the livery of the supposed new owners.

Computer frauds are usually divided into two classes: user fraud and technical fraud. Technical fraud includes all those instances requiring computing skills such as knowledge of programming. Program and system modification frauds fall into this category. Although such frauds are fascinating they are comparatively rare, and most known instances of computer fraud follow classic patterns. Fraudulent input documents require much lower levels of skill. The records show that the old tricks still work. In fact there is some likelihood that traditional controls tend to lapse as computer systems are introduced, especially in small- to medium-sized installations. Segregation of duties is hard to achieve if there are fewer staff than there were in the traditional clerical system. The very flexibility of computer-based systems encourages a merging of duties so that staff tend to cover more aspects of a job like sales order processing. Attitude is important also.

There is a tendency to assume that the necessary controls are incorporated somehow into the computer system. This is especially so with small business systems. Such an assumption is unwarranted, and managements should check that appropriate controls exist in the total corporate system.

There is also an almost childlike faith in computer print-out. Any competent programmer can change a program so that it produces any output that he desires. The output may bear no relation to the input data supplied to the program. The programmer could arrange to suppress printing and totalling of particular kinds of records – say for particular accounts or payroll numbers. Never believe uncorroborated evidence of a print-out. The Equity Funding scandal which was the subject of the BBC television programme 'The Billion Dollar Bubble' would have collapsed sooner if people had demanded confirmation that the policies listed by the computer did in fact exist.

Many opportunities for fraud arise from poor systems design. The 80:20 rule so often applies. The computer system copes with almost all the cases. This is usually easy, because the bulk of transactions can be handled relatively easily. It is all the peculiar ones that cause the trouble. Classic examples are payment of contract workers, not on the payroll, or payments to a few overseas suppliers in foreign currencies. The original manual systems had routines for handling all these things. Often the fault arises from poor specification. The potential user frequently defines only half the problem, because he does not believe the computer system will do everything. This is a real problem, because managers sometimes do not know how complex the real world is.

The fraud opportunities arise because the manual system with its controls has virtually disappeared. One person is frequently trusted to sort out all the odd problems, with no segregation of duties. The person concerned is usually very capable and well thought of.

A UK packaging manufacturer ran into problems paying for imports of board and paper from his suppliers in Sweden. The exchange rate was fluctuating, and the computer payments system was in a mess. The firm took on a temporary accountant to sort out the problems. He was good, and soon things were happy once again. The accountant was given authority to draw relatively large cheques – business was booming, and trade was good. There were some questions at the annual audit, but he explained away duplicate cheques by losses in the post. After three years he had drawn £218,000, and cleared the cheques into local accounts opened in the same names as those of the suppliers in Sweden. He was caught because he attempted to overdraw one of the accounts as he was preparing his get-away. The company published full details of the case as a warning to others.

Many lessons can be learnt. The opportunity arose because of limitations of the normal payment system. The individual was given too much authority with little or no control. The firm did not apply its usual recruitment checking process. It took the man on a temporary basis, and then transferred him to permanent staff. Had it followed up references in normal fashion, it would have discovered that the man was in prison when he claimed to be working in Canada.

The account of disposal of the money is interesting, especially the item 'To purchase of second Lotus sports car . . .'. Another point to bear in mind is that one can open a bank account in almost any name one likes. Few companies these days examine cleared cheques. Had this firm done so for what were very large payments, it would have discovered that they were presented locally instead of in Sweden.

In 1977 a female salaries officer was jailed at Winchester Crown Court. She pleaded guilty to 13 fraud charges (and asked for 67 others to be taken into account). She had the option of paying doctors' expenses by hand-written cheque or through the automatic system at the Hampshire Area Health Authority computer. Her fiddle was to pay the doctors via the computer and to pay to her own account hand-written cheques for the same expenses. Over a period of 2 years she amassed £12,000 in this way to augment her £250 monthly salary.

Many similar cases are on record. Lack of adequate control is a major factor. Input frauds are quite common. In a £230,000 fraud, authorised invoices were originally input for payment to valid suppliers' accounts. Subsequently they were reinput by the fraudster to fictitious suppliers' accounts bearing identical references and values, except for account numbers. Cheques were then signed by the authorised signatories for the valid and the fictitious supplier payments. The fictitious payment cheques were then withdrawn and paid to the bank. The critical weakness is that the fraudster was able to handle both the input and the cheques produced. Moreover the authorised signatories did not insist on documentation to support the payments.

The emergency payments system was circumvented by a senior establishments officer in a £5166 fraud. During staff absences, such as lunchtime or sickness, he prepared cheques and entered the cash book. Some payments were duplicates of genuine payments and some were refunds due to, but not paid to, former employees. He prepared the input forms for the computer payroll and allocated payments to the non-taxable head. The computer system did not accumulate such non-taxable payments, so no permanent record was kept. This was changed after discovery of the fraud, and non-taxable pay is now accumulated and printed on pay slips. Any unusual amounts thus shown may alert employees. Senior staff do not now have access to cheques, and are instructed not to write up the cash book.

These examples illustrate the need for constant vigilance. Those who use a system have ample opportunity to study it, even to explore it for weaknesses. One can be sure that someone will eventually seek out and exploit any that exist. Computer systems are only as effective as the environment allows.

Quite often a user at a terminal accidentally discovers that something unexpectedly works. Some accident reveals a new transaction type, perhaps by a typing mistake. Curiosity may prompt the user to explore a little further. One of three things may happen. The user may not appreciate the significance of the discovery, and may simply ignore it. An intelligent and alert person may realise the potential, and report it. Depending on motivation and honesty there is thirdly the possibility of fraud.

One area of considerable difficulty is control of program libraries and of systems programming in general. If possible there should be total separation between production libraries and program development. Development programmers should never be allowed access to production data even as copies for test purposes. All production work and associated media should be protected against unauthorised access by non-production staff. This is a counsel of perfection, and may be impossible to achieve in a small site.

There is the problem of emergency maintenance when a production suite fails out-of-hours. Very commonly a systems programmer is on call to fix it. How is such work monitored and controlled? If there is a proper password system to limit access to various application systems, the systems programmer will need access to fix the problem. How do you monitor and control this, and perhaps change the password next day? One interesting approach was to print the password details on slips inside envelopes of the sort often used for payroll or interest notifications. These were held under lock and key, and use of the password meant that the envelope had to be unsealed.

All controls cost money or convenience. One must balance the risk of fraud against other adverse factors of the control measures. This might be increased cost of working, or loss of responsiveness to customers.

Controls in computer systems can be better and more consistent than those existing in comparable manual systems. It is possible to use part of the enormous power of the system to monitor and record what is going on. Not only this, but the records can be analysed looking for unusual or significant patterns that may indicate potential fraud or other malpractice.

The usual technique is to write each transaction to a system journal, which is maintained by the computer operating system. Every transaction is recorded together with its time of entry, and the identity of the operator. Such a journal can be relatively compact, and it can be processed automatically by audit staff. There is an additional benefit if people who access the system know that their actions are recorded, and will be inspected as a matter of course. It is fairly simple to generate details of each transaction within the system. The main difficulty is to ensure that the operator's identity is known. So far as possible, people should have unique access keys of whatever sort (passwords, badges, etc) rather than shared ones. If several people need to access an application they should have separate passwords or badges. It is then much harder for an individual to masquerade as a colleague.

All attempted violations of the transaction rules should be investigated. If there are many it implies that the rules are misunderstood, or that confusion occurs between transaction types. Some refinement is needed to bring the numbers down, so that the records are worth investigating. There is no point in maintaining records and controls if there is no discipline. If routines are sloppy and errors are unchecked, carelessness can lead to fraud and dishonesty.

Discrepancies in one sales ledger system were ascribed to computer error. The company had relatively poor controls anyway, so no one was very concerned. When someone complained that his account had not been credited with payments made, the company blamed computer errors. A new auditor, concerned at the general attitude, examined the pattern of errors.

He found that there was a crop of them about the middle of each month, when one or two large payments apparently disappeared. Investigation showed that a terminal operator was in collusion with a customer. She selected two or three payments each month – perhaps $8000 to $10,000 – and credited them to her friend's account. She then phoned to advise him of the net balance needed to settle the account.

The losses were not large in terms of the total operation, but they had been accepted in a climate of lax control, and almost of indifference to safeguarding of corporate assets.

Fraud is just one example of deliberate misuse. Use of computer time for non-company purposes is another. Several cases of private bureaux operated on company computers are on record both here and in the States. It is hard to prove theft in such cases in this country. Wise managements ban all private use of computer resources as part of their personnel policies. It is so easy for casual help for a friend to grow until it interferes with legitimate work. Private use may impose a significant load on the system leading to real increased costs.

Malicious damage is unfortunately common. Many fires are probably started deliberately, and arson must always be considered. Deliberate fires are sometimes not intended to cause major damage. A security guard was seeking promotion, but there were few opportunities to demonstrate his skills. He 'discovered' a small fire in an office during the evening, and put it out. In his third attempt, the fire took hold, causing massive damage and disruption.

In Italy, France and West Germany there have been terrorist attacks on computers. The Red Brigade in Italy destroyed communications processors at eleven major installations. Average loss was $500,000. They produced a document, Resolutions of the Strategic Directorate, that depicts increased use of computers as part of a plot to maximise social controls. It describes computers as instruments of the class struggle, and claims that it is important to attack, unravel and destroy these networks of control. In France, politically motivated attacks were mounted against computers, which were seen as a symbol of capitalist oppression. Organisations were attacked simply because they had a computer.

Computer systems are vulnerable to all kinds of deliberate threats. A computer installation represents a valuable concentration of resources, relative to other office services. The value of equipment per square foot is very high. Moreover the equipment is relatively delicate. It needs a special environment – air conditioning, 'clean' power supplies, and so on.

Not only is the computer valuable, but it is often vital for the business. Very many corporate systems are dependent upon continued availability of the computer. The trade unions have been quick to recognise this. Particular classes of work have been 'blacked'. Obvious candidates have been sales invoices. The telephone billing system was brought to a standstill as part of a dispute. Most subscribers received at least six months free credit for rentals. At the end of the dispute about £1000 million was unbilled.

The vulnerable systems are those concerned with cash flow or customer service. Except in a monopoly situation customer loyalty cannot be guaranteed. Changes in business practices over recent years have increased vulnerability. Stocks are much lower, and timescales much shorter; the effects of disruption are seen quickly.

High street retailing provides an example. One firm found that shelves would be noticeably bare after a few days' disruption of its computer-based warehouse and distribution system. Housewives would probably go to a competitor in such an event. Winning them back may not be easy.

The range of possible deliberate attacks is limited only by human ingenuity. Threats from people must be taken seriously. Motivation is important. Why should someone attack your installation? Who might be motivated to do so? Can you identify likely perpetrators and their motives?

Jay BloomBecker at the Los Angeles based National Centre for Computer Crime Data has come up with some profiles. Many computer criminals are not clever; their crimes are not technically sophisticated. Environment not personality is the deciding factor. The criminal's view of the computer system is significant, and it may not accord with our view of that same system. Some views are irrational or even bizarre.

The two most interesting of BloomBecker's seven views are the playpen and the war zone.

The computer is seen as a playpen or even a toy by many students. Professor John Carroll found that 34 per cent of students on two courses on advanced information systems tried to obtain computer time without paying for it. The same proportion tried to penetrate the computer's security system at the University of Western Ontario.

Stanley Rifkin pleaded guilty to charges of obtaining £5.1 million from an American Bank. Rifkin accidentally saw the daily codes used by the bank to authenticate fund transfer messages. On impulse he sent a transfer, and used the resulting funds to buy diamonds. He failed to hide the diamonds and was dumbfounded when arrested. He claimed that this was the first indication he had that his impulsive scheme had really worked. His actions were inept. He failed to plan for converting the stolen sum. The diamond market is suspicious when someone unknown arrives with large quantities. It is probable that Rifkin effected the fraudulent transfer just to see if it would work. It was an experiment, to see what would happen.

These kinds of attempts arise from failure to define clearly what is permitted and what is off-limits in connection with a computer system. The fantastic growth in the personal computer market demonstrates that using a computer is extremely satisfying. Solving puzzles is a fine way of passing the time. Computer systems can be seen as a game. It can be fun to check the supposed limits. Is it really so difficult to access the password file?

In business systems, management must define the limits of what is allowable. Private and unauthorised use of corporate systems leads to all kinds of problems. It is best prohibited.

Disgruntled employees often see the computer as a route for revenge against their employer. This has been called the 'warzone' view. A classic example occurred at a US soft drinks manufacturer. After a dispute they dismissed a delivery driver. Unfortunately they overlooked the fact that the employee's financée was their tape librarian. She was incensed by their action. Over a few weeks she replaced the main master files by virgin tapes, properly labelled of course. When several generations were blank she quit her job. Interestingly, she readily found employment in the next state since her experience was so good.

In Sacramento, California, three employees of the State Department of Justice were upset by what they regarded as a miserly pay rise. They deleted certain records of arrest in the criminal record files. There are lots of similar cases. Sometimes employees have deliberately sabotaged equipment.

The best defence here is to create better employee relations by fair personnel policies. So far as possible, duties should be split so that no one person has total control over a media library for instance. This may be difficult in a small installation. Certified back-up copies of vital data should be held off-site for contingency planning reasons. They might also serve as a safeguard against malicious destruction.

Staff attitude is very important in prevention of fraud. A survey of attitudes to propriety in the US showed that people could be divided very roughly into three groups. Only one quarter of the people were strictly honest. Another quarter were quite openly dishonest – they would steal anything that they could lay hands on, without considering the consequences. The other half were opportunists. They would steal if they felt they could get away with it. What this means is that in a cross-section of the population only 1 in 4 can be relied upon.

The first step in a fraud prevention programme must be to get rid of the dishonest people. There are cases on record where an entire workforce has been in collusion. In one such case there were 125 people involved.

Having eliminated the baddies, one must gain support of the honest folk. A security programme must have their support, and the security measures should not alienate their sympathies. Often this is a matter of presentation and good staff relations. Having secured their support one must attempt to win support from the waverers in the middle group. Peer group influence and management attitude are very important. If there is a casual attitude to company resources at the top, this is sure to filter down the organisation.

Fraud potential is a feature of almost every job. It is not necessary to have access to cash. Opportunity varies with rank, access and skills. The evidence is that people stick to their own sphere. Payroll clerks tend to perpetrate only payroll frauds. They do not as a rule venture into sales frauds. Fraudsters usually justify their actions to themselves. They rationalise their activity, and may have either an economic or a psychological need to commit the fraud.

Fraud is more likely where there is low chance of detection coupled with leniency if the action is detected. It is unfortunate that companies tend not to prosecute today. It is simpler, and far cheaper to accept the individual's resignation rather than go for prosecution. This may allow a fraudster to go on and repeat the offence elsewhere. Many companies skip proper vetting of applicants for employment, and fail to take up references even when these are supplied.

Once a computer system is employed it may be very hard to secure satisfactory legal evidence to secure conviction. The defence in a criminal case merely have to show reasonable doubt about the evidence, whereas the prosecution need an almost perfect case. From this it follows that operating procedures and standards have to be above reproach. Adequate records must be maintained to show that the computer system was properly maintained and that the supposed fraudulent transactions could not have been created in some other way, by machine fault or maloperation.

The case of Pettigrew is important because the admissibility of automatically generated computer evidence was considered by the English courts. The case concerned a burglary in the North of England. Some money was stolen from a house. It consisted of £650 in new £5 notes that the victim had obtained from the local bank. The police arrested Mr Stuart Pettigrew, who had in his possession some notes that bore serial numbers that might have indicated that they came from the same batch of notes given to the victim. The prosecution tried to put in evidence a print-out from the Bank of England computer indicating that these notes were part of a batch passed to the bank and into the possession of the victim. At appeal it was argued that the print-out was not admissible because the information had been generated by machine action alone. Pettigrew was acquitted.

The assumption is that uncorroborated computer evidence is not now admissible in criminal cases.

The final problem is what to do if a fraud is discovered. Corporate management must establish clear policy on this issue before the event. Even if there is clear 'evidence' this may be insufficient to bring a prosecution. Excellent guidance is contained in a small book from the CIPFA. Everyone who might encounter evidence of fraud should read this or a similar work so that they are prepared.

The police should be contacted informally at the earliest stage if there is any intention to prosecute. Secrecy is vital, and preliminary meetings might take place on neutral ground. The job of the police is to prepare a case for prosecution, not to unravel the details from your accounting system. Each of the 41 Police Forces in England and Wales has a Fraud Squad or Divisional Detectives trained in fraud investigation. Training of officers is being strengthened, to equip them to handle computer related crime. Typical advice from the police is not to interview a suspect unless absolutely sure of your ground. Only those with a 'need to know' should be involved. Anything may be vital evidence. Organisations lose as much by human error as they do from fraud; if in doubt, seek advice.

A decision to prosecute may be hard to make. Preparing a case is tiresome and very expensive, and may cause disruption for the company's normal operations. Bringing the case to court will usually involve the police. Their job is not to establish the fraud but to prepare a case. The police have ready access to specialist forensic services not readily available in the ordinary way. Officers in fraud squads are primarily policemen rather than accountants or computer experts. Investigation and preparation of a case will involve significant company resources. If the case comes to court several staff are likely to have to attend as witnesses, perhaps waiting for days or even weeks. The cost in time may run into thousands of pounds. For what? Success is not certain. Only about half of all fraud prosecutions result in conviction, and one assumes that the police only bring to court those cases that they consider worthwhile.

9 Risk Management

Many events pose threats to an organisation or to its computer systems. Risk management provides an approach to handling the problem of how to deal with such threats. There are three stages or facets in the process. First the risks must be identified, then their impact must be assessed or analysed, and thirdly the risks must be handled in some way.

Risk management is a corporate responsibility. The organisation should appoint a risk manager with the necessary authority to carry out the task. The broad aim of risk management is to produce and implement a plan or programme of countermeasures in the best interests of the organisation. In small organisations risk management might be necessarily a part-time function. In large, complex ones a team will be needed. The time needed, and the level and breadth of experience required mean that significant resources are consumed. The risk manager would normally lead any risk management team. He needs direct reporting lines to top management. A balanced view is needed. The risk manager or his team needs access at minimum to organisational components responsible for the following:

DP Operations Management

Systems Programming

Internal Audit

Physical/Site Security

Data Files and Applications Support

It is important to separate the function of team leader from that of representative. So, for instance, in a small organisation the risk management team leader might come from one of the first three groups. In such a case that function ought also to be represented. Other departments and functions, such as legal and personnel should at least be consulted if not represented.

When management establishes the risk management function it should leave members of the organisation in no doubt about the scope of the team, and the fact that it will rely upon the findings.

The leader and team members should be designated in writing. Their responsibilities, duties and authority should also be specified in writing. It should be made clear that the job cannot be done properly if alternates are assigned to the task. Sometimes teams tend to collect more information than is necessary, thus prolonging the task needlessly. The risk management tasks are as follows:

— gathering information about the organisation: what it does, how it operates, its assets and resources;

— identifying the risks to these assets and resources, and assessing them, their impact and likely frequency;

— identifying countermeasures to these risks, their costs, and likely effectiveness;

— preparing security programmes and submitting them to management;

— preparing plans for implementing authorised security programmes;

— monitoring and reviewing the effectiveness of these programmes.

The process is not a static one. The organisation changes, as does the world outside. The risks that are faced and the losses to be expected will change with time.

It is important to study the organisation at the outset as a preliminary to the actual risk analysis. Is the organisation likely to be a special target for some reason? Has it special resources? One output from the preliminary analysis should be a listing of all the assets of the organisation with best estimates of current replacement cost. Another should be a list of any special threats to the organisation, any special vulnerabilities. The third is a note of special resources and existing countermeasures. The listing of asset costs gives the best estimate of the need for security in the organisation.

Risk identification is the process of systematically discovering as many as possible of the risks to which the system is exposed. A systematic approach is desirable, otherwise items will be overlooked.

One should consider carefully all the assets and resources, and for each one think of possible ways in which loss might be caused. In other words what are the risks to this asset or resource? What could adversely affect it? The complementary approach can also be tried. One can consider the various factors that may contribute to loss, such as natural disasters, special local hazards, unauthorised entry, power supply failure, employee unrest, and so on. Understanding these factors can contribute substantially to the risk identification process. Various published sources can be used to assist, by pointing out other elements that should be considered by the risk management team.

Identification of threats is done using a combination of methods involving the use of *checklists, flowcharts* and *financial statements*.

Checklists are available in many publications. To be of most use to the risk manager the checklist should contain lists of threats or questions such as 'Is your system adequately protected against (specific named threat)?'. Some checklists are less helpful in that they identify countermeasures rather than threats.

A second technique is to use flowcharts, especially in an industrial environment. A flowchart shows inputs, processes and outputs and the relationship between them, and between suppliers, factories, distributors and consumers. The effect upon outputs of non-availability of a raw material or a process can be determined from a flowchart. Similarly in a computer-based system, flowcharts can be used to assist in identifying the various threats to security.

A configuration diagram for the hardware, including the communication system, and the physical connections between units is useful. Similarly a flow diagram for each suite of programs can help to identify vulnerability. For each system there should be a system flowchart showing the relationships between the normal processes, the computer processes and the transmission of data.

The financial statements of the organisation can be used to identify how much income can be attributed to each product or service, and how much it costs to support each one. The balance sheet will reveal the values of fixed (and current) assets.

A procedure for threat identification is described by Dr K K Wong in *Risk Analysis and Control* (NCC Publications). Twelve vulnerable areas are identified within an organisation which has computing systems:

— nature of business, objectives;

— economic environment;

— physical environment;

— supply of essential services;

— company structure;

— organisation chart;

— structure of dp functions (physical siting);

— flow of information inside dp department;

— flow of information between dp and user departments;

— assets: supply, replacement and management;

— in-house dp services;

— direct services to public.

For each of these areas there is a threat analysis chart, tabulating the threats and means of identifying the threats (and a list of possible countermeasures as well).

Having identified the risks (or at least the more obvious ones!), the next stage is to analyse the potential impact of these risks. The two important elements of risk analysis are an assessment of the damage or loss that might be caused by an event, and the likely frequency of the event. How often might it happen in a period of time?

Clearly, exact information will not be available either for the impact or the frequency. Fortunately this does not matter. An educated guess is sufficiently accurate for the assessment. The assessments must be made on the basis of historical evidence, the team's special knowledge and experience, and any other data available to them.

Estimates to an order of magnitude are quite sufficient, both for frequency and loss.

Money is the yardstick used to measure loss. Inconvenience, embarrassment and other intangibles are important factors; but they are not easily quantified. You have to put a value on the impact or loss. How many customers, and therefore sales might be lost? The value selected is the expected loss as a result of the occurrence. It is a best estimate based on the data available.

The normal currency unit (pound, dollars, etc) is used for the estimate. The impact need only be measured or estimated within factors of ten. The estimate might be £11000 or £14000 but a figure of £10000 will do. The scale might run 10, 100, 1000, 10000, etc, to say 100 million. Any estimate is an approximation.

The frequency of an event is hard to measure, but estimates can be made. Some threats occur only once in a number of years, others several times a day. A year is a convenient base for estimates of likely frequency. 'Once in five years' converts to 'one fifth of an occurrence per year'. Similarly twice a day converts to '730 times a year'. A useful scale is 'once in 300 years', 'once in 30 years', changing by a factor of 10 at each step. Three years is about 1000 days, which gives the convenient scale shown below.

Impact £ or $

If impact is		
	10	let index i = 1
	100	2
	1000	3
	10,000	4
	100,000	5
	1 million	6
	10 million	7
	100 million	8

Frequency

If frequency is once in 300 years, let f	=	1
30		2
3		3
100 days		4
10		5
1		6
10 times/day		7
100		8

The tables show convenient scales for both impact and frequency. Three years is roughly 1000 days, so the scale is also in decimal multiples. The index I and frequency F can be used to calculate the annual loss exposure, and Table 1 allows this to be done directly.

The annual loss exposure is a measure of the relative importance of a particular element. If the impact of an event (the amount of loss or damage it would cause) and the frequency of occurrence (number of times per year) could be specified, the product of the two would be a statement of the loss, or:

Loss = Impact x Frequency of Occurrence

The two factors cannot be specified exactly but an approximation is the annual loss exposure (ALE) which is the product of the estimated impact (I) and the estimated frequency of occurrence per year (F). When i and f are indexes to the possible orders of impact and frequency, the relationship between i and I is $I = 10^i$ and the relationship of f to F is:

$$F = \frac{10^f}{3000} \quad \text{or} \quad F = \frac{10^{(f-3)}}{3}$$

The annual loss expectancy is:

ALE = I x F

$$= 10^i \; x \; \frac{10^{f-3}}{3} \; = \; \frac{10^{(f + i-3)}}{3}$$

Impact £ or $	Frequency → i= \ f=	Once in 300 years (100,000 days) **1**	Once in 30 years (10,000 days) **2**	Once in 3 years (1000 days) **3**	Once in 100 days **4**	Once in 10 days **5**	Once per day **6**	10 times per day **7**
10	1					300	3000	30K
100	2				300	3000	30K	300K
1000	3			300	3000	30K	300K	3M
10,000	4		300	3000	30K	300K	3M	30M
100,000	5	300	3000	30K	300K	3M	30M	
1,000,000	6	3000	30K	300K	3M	30M		
10,000,000	7	30K	300K	3M	30M			
100,000,000	8	300K	3M	30M				

Table 1

Table 1 can be used to find the ALE. The appropriate row and column are selected. Where they intersect gives the ALE.

The threat severity matrix (Figure 1) is a useful tool for thinking about risks and losses. A particular risk is entered somewhere in the matrix according to the size of loss and the expected frequency. The frequency scale increases from left to right, and the expected loss from top to bottom. The matrix is very like the table used for finding annual loss exposures.

Events with the same ALE lie on a diagonal from bottom left to top right. Notice particularly that these are not events of the same kind. Those at the top right represent steady, regular but small losses. They are the common everyday losses due to minor errors or omissions. They are rather like a leaking bucket, in that they constitute a steady drain on the organisation. Those at the opposite end of this diagonal, at the bottom left, are very infrequent events. They are likely to be disasters if they should occur. They are more like someone kicking over the bucket, or even breaching the dam wall.

Risks plotted at the top left are usually ignored, but one ought to be cautious about accepting them without question. Some check or audit should be made of all losses, to ensure that they really are accidental. Baird (in Ellison, 1981) gives an excellent account of a situation where a casual attitude to such errors existed. In fact it concealed a web of computer fraud.

Events plotted at the bottom of the matrix represent disasters waiting to happen. These risks are usually transferred by insurance or contract. A risk plotted in the bottom right is not tolerable. No one could afford to take on such risks.

Having considered the possible risks, assessed their likelihood and the possible consequences, attention must be given to handling them and dealing with the situation. There are four ways of handling risks: some may be avoided, and others may be retained, reduced or transferred.

Sometimes a risk can be avoided by altering the method of working or operation in some way. Other risks can be avoided by dispensing with some particular service, facility or item of equipment. This may be voluntary, or essential because the risk cannot

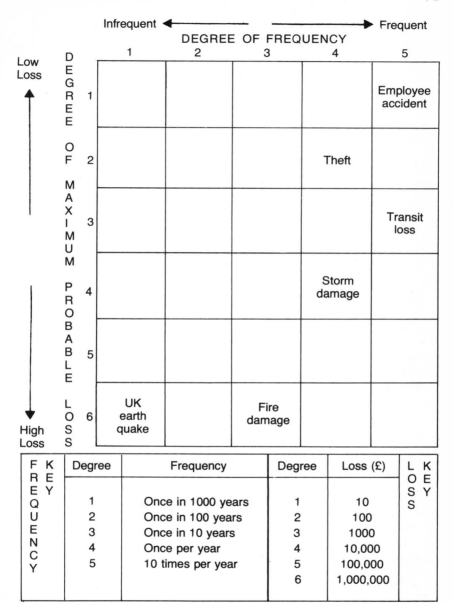

Figure 1   Threat Severity Matrix

be reduced or eliminated in any other way. If avoidance is selected as a way of handling a particular risk it is vital to exercise vigilance in the future to prevent reintroduction of the risk. This is one example of the need for continuous review. Any change in circumstances, internal or external, may introduce new risks or uncover old ones once again.

Another valid way of handling risk is retention. If the risk would have only minor consequences it might be carried by the organisation. The expected loss for such risks would be small and it could be handled without embarrassment. The organisation may accept retention of risks having low cost but high frequency of occurrence. It may not be sensible to accept retention of those with high cost but low frequency of occurrence. In the threat security matrix chart (Figure 1) these two kinds of risk tend to be located in opposite corners. The low-frequency/high-cost ones are at the bottom left. Potentially they are disasters. The low-cost/high-frequency ones are at the top right, and are often accepted by organisations.

The point is that the organisation can accept a steady low cost. It may not be able to accept a risk with identical annual loss exposure if that risk is a very low-frequency but high-cost event, ie a disaster.

Conscious deliberate retention of identified risks must not be confused with unwitting retention due to failure to identify the risk – a failure that could have very embarrassing consequences.

The third way of handling risk is, for example, reduction by use of countermeasures. Countermeasures usually add to expense, but may not do so if they are simply changes in procedures.

There are two ways in which risks may be transferred: insurance and contract. Insurance can provide some financial recompense for losses which occur. The annual cost of premiums is known in advance. Insurance is complicated by the exclusion of the first part of any claim by 'excess' clauses. This means that the insured retains part of the risk. Some risks can be transferred by contract such as warranty or maintenance agreements. Standby arrangements are a typical example. Obviously the organisation accepting the contractual risk must be reputable.

The effectiveness of countermeasures can be estimated. Two values can be associated with any particular countermeasure. The first is the cost expressed over the same period as the expected loss. The costs of development, implementation, operation and maintenance should be included. The second value is the effectiveness of the countermeasure in reducing the frequency or the financial loss (impact) of the occurrence of the risk. This can be difficult, but the best available estimate should be used.

The effectiveness might be expressed as a factor E in the range 0 to 1.0 by which the countermeasure reduces the expected loss – the greater the effectiveness, the lower the expected loss. For instance, if a countermeasure has an effectiveness $E = 0.75$, the expected loss would be reduced by this factor to 0.25 of its original value.

The total expected cost associated with a particular risk allowing for the effects of a countermeasure is as follows:

Total expected annual cost =
Expected annual loss exposure (1–E) +
annual costs of countermeasure

A countermeasure is only effective economically if it produces a reduction in annual loss exposure greater than its own annual costs.

Risks may be considered in order of decreasing annual loss exposure. There may be a case for considering disasters first of all. One should examine first of all those risks with associated loss of unacceptable size, too great for the organisation to bear. Each risk is examined in turn. For each risk new values of expected loss and total expected cost can be calculated.

The aim of risk management is to select that set of countermeasures that has a lower total expected cost than any other set. Some combinations may be excluded by financial or legal constraints. For example, a particular programme of countermeasures may be considered to be too expensive by corporate management. Money spent on security measures has to be found by the organisation. There is always competition for resources, and the management may decide as a business risk to devote resources to developing a new product or building a new facility. The job of corporate management is to take such decisions. The risk management team must make sure that such decisions are taken with full knowledge, properly presented.

10 Contingency Planning

Data processing staff at the Hertford Insurance in the United States were surprised one day at being called to a special staff meeting. The Director announced to the staff that the local tape vaults had been destroyed in a simulated fire. As an exercise the staff were assigned the task of sorting out a recovery plan in just three hours. Their assignment was to show how they were going to recover the applications systems from the effects of the simulated fire. One condition was that all the on-site media and documentation were irrecoverably lost. The problem, therefore, was how to bring these applications back to the state they had been in just before-hand. No pre-warning of the exercise was given. In reporting the experiment, the company said that they learnt a great deal.

Many data processing people would be shattered if faced with this sort of exercise.

Real disasters are fairly common, so some planning is needed. It need not be a fire or a flood or some physical disaster that causes you to go into extended back-up working. At one site, NCC had a mutual back-up arrangement with another similar ICL site. Our machine, an ICL 1900 series running George 3 became virtually unusable because of apparent controller errors, which caused system crashes. The local engineers failed to solve this problem even with a very high level of support from the manufacturer. We were forced into back-up working, first of all for evening shift; then through the night for one night. Then the following night, and the following weekend, until eventually we were taking all the time that we could get on the other site to run our own work and our customers' work. We ran a bureau service. We were doing this night after night for many weeks. Trials had been done in advance on both sites to make sure that we could run our applications there. We did this on a regular basis. Each quarter we would take an application across and run it one weekend.

Even though we had done such trials and tests, many of our applications failed for trivial reasons, because things like fundamental utilities that we had on our libraries were not available in quite the same state on the other site. We had made assumptions about the site that were not true but were, we assumed, general practice. We thought that what we did was normal, but we found to our cost, that this was not the case in actual practice.

In a period of about eight weeks working in this way, we discovered how very hard it is to maintain morale. Initially when you go into this sort of back-up working everyone is excited. A sort of euphoria extends to it because you are facing a challenge. Spirits are high, but after a few days people get tired. Very hard work on the part of all concerned produces less than satisfactory service to your end users.

The work was very demanding. When we went on site at perhaps midnight, we had to restore the file store on disk or at least do a partial restore to bring ourselves up to date. The equipment was not quite the same as our own, so things like identifiers for peripherals were different. Our experienced operators, shift leaders and so on were quite happy, but junior staff lacked the confidence on a foreign site that they had at home. They were scared to do things that they would do at home, or to take risks because they were not familiar with the equipment.

The initial euphoria soon wears off. Tiredness among staff becomes obvious. Not only that, but when the operations people get back home, the users in effect, blame the computer staff for the deficiencies. Although these people are working very hard, their end users do not see just how hard they are working, and what efforts they are putting in to try and achieve these results, because most of the action is elsewhere. Lack of corporate management support is always something of a problem, because management also tend not to appreciate the problems for similar reasons.

What then do we mean by contingency planning? A useful definition is that a contingency is an unscheduled interruption of data processing capability. The contingency is unscheduled. It is an event that causes unscheduled interruption to data processing capability; something that causes you to do things that you do not do as part and parcel of your daily operations.

Contingency planning is devising ways for coping with the effects of such an interruption. Why should you have any contingencies of this kind? You always have residual risks in any security program. This is partly because the countermeasures that you have obtained are not totally effective against the risks that you have identified. The countermeasures are not a complete defence. You can never achieve perfection, but even when you have done realistic risk analysis, you will always have risks which you have not identified. Perhaps you have risks for which you have no countermeasures whatever. Therefore, there will always be a chance that you will have some contingency, some possible disaster waiting to happen.

There are two aspects to contingency planning. The more obvious one is stand-by planning, that is planning for an alternative facility to replace the normal data processing one. There is also the other aspect, often overlooked, which is recovery planning. How do you manage to get back to normal from your stand-by mode of working? How do you find enough resources, enough money to recover your normal operation, when you are probably stretched to the utmost trying to run your stand-by facility? Recovery is vitally important because very hard efforts in stand-by working produce less than satisfactory service. Your already stretched people are getting tired, you have not enough of them, and the key people that you need to do recovery are probably already fully occupied doing the stand-by operation. You must have proper planning for both aspects, stand-by and recovery.

Contingency planning is *not* a problem for data processing management. Lots of DPMs assume that it is their problem. They are wrong. It is a corporate problem. Data processing management cannot solve back-up planning by themselves. That cannot be emphasised too strongly. The problem is one for the organisation. Top management must be made aware of the sorts of risks that are faced, and the sorts of consequences that may follow. If you have a real disaster and you are very dependent on computing facilities, the whole organisation may be at risk. A disaster may cause bankruptcy or the loss of customer goodwill. If top management support is missing, then in my view, you cannot sensibly do contingency planning. If you do not have corporate support then you will not have sufficient resources to solve the problems. You need to bring in more people than you would have available in normal circumstances to run a computing facility. You need to bring in other skills, administrative, legal skills and so on. If you do not have support from the organisation to bring those skills to bear in face of disaster, then the organisation as a whole is not responding as it should. You must mobilise these resources at the outset of planning.

Any planning team trying to do contingency planning should be kept small. Four or five people is about the right number to be involved in a team. You obviously need somebody from data processing, having both breadth, and technical knowledge to appreciate the problems. It is very useful to have someone representing the company secretary or legal departments, with abilities to solve external problems. If you can find somebody from estates or building or site security, who is concerned with physical things on the ground, that brings complementary skills. Somebody from either internal audit or finance can bring other knowledge to bear on the problems. Finally if you can involve a user, then you have probably got a reasonable balance in the team.

One of the first things that such a team ought to do is to try to get classification of the applications that are run. The users should be asked to classify the relative importance of the different applications in a disaster situation. These may be quite different from their normal relative importances.

You could classify applications into three priority levels.

First, as priority one, there are those that are essential to keep the organisation alive. These may not be the ones that are regarded as vital and important in normal times. Usually these top-priority applications are concerned with maintaining cash flow, or with some aspect of customer satisfaction or customer service.

In priority level two are classified all the less important things, where a delay of weeks or even months may be acceptable. And finally you have those systems or applications in priority-three which are discretionary. The organisation can survive without the information that is provided by these priority-three applications.

It is a fundamental mistake to assume that back-up means that you can run normal service somewhere else. If you try to replicate your existing facility on some other site, or in some other way, then you will find that it is far too expensive. You will certainly have to reduce the level of operation that you are seeking to achieve.

What sort of plans should be produced from the contingency planning exercise? As a rule you need what are called Cascade Plans. The vital need is to delegate as speedily as possible in the face of disaster. The first stage of the plan must always be to call up extra people, to call in nominated people (or their alternates) to carry out the second and subsequent stages of the plan. If the man on the spot tries to solve the problem himself, he will fall flat on his face. He simply has insufficient resources. The first stage of the plan must therefore be to delegate. It must call in more people. When these people arrive they are given their delegated piece of the plan. They know what to do and how to take things further.

So, the first level of your cascade plan entails getting more people together, mobilisation of resources and delegation. As soon as the new people arrive, they begin to execute another piece of the plan, so that more and more resources are brought in to solve the problems. These stage-two people probably do much the same thing. They probably call in or notify more people, both internal and external, to bring adequate resources to bear on the problem. If the early people simply try to solve the problem themselves, they will be far less likely to succeed.

In considering your plan you have to think about the sorts of contingency that might arise for your own operation. The response may have to differ according to the kinds of things that could happen; response to a flood might be totally different to the response to a fire. If the disaster is nearby, a neighbourhood disaster, your operation may be physically unaffected. There may be no damage, but it may be that you have no access to the site even though it is undamaged and everything is still there. There is no question of loss on the site, but there is the real question of how do you operate somewhere else? Consider who could possibly help.

Establish contact with the likely people at a high level, before the disaster. Try to secure cooperation and in particular try to get out-of-hours contacts. Disasters have a habit of happening on a Sunday evening on a bank holiday weekend. You must have ways of contacting the right people in your own and other organisations at such times. You must have private telephone numbers available, as well as the golf club number and so on. You need names and alternates; if you cannot raise the Managing Director, who is going to stand in for him? You need addresses for things like services, all kinds of supplies, transportation, who is going to provide the food, accommodation, hotels, catering, endless lists of additional suppliers. If you contacted them beforehand it is usually quite easy to arrange that they will provide these things without purchase orders if the contingency should arise. But if you try to do this at the last minute when disaster has struck, there will be difficulties.

Going back to the applications that you chose and selected as priority one, proper design of those applications for stand-by working is essential. Applications should have plenty of recovery points in them, far more then you would normally expect to use. It may be that your stand-by facility is smaller than your own and runs at lower speed. Suites very often run almost to completion and then something breaks at the last minute. If you do not have restart points in those suites then on the back-up site you have to go right back to the beginning and re-run the whole system. Much time can be lost in that way.

Again, consider that normal data control facilities may be missing. In the early stages of disaster recovery you probably will not have your normal data control facilities available, because you are say, 50 miles away. You cannot transport all the people and all the documentation to the back-up site. Quite a lot of things may be lost because of the lack of data control in and out that normally occurs. You may get mistakes that would not pass into operations in normal times, because people are not there to check for them. So how shall you cope with that?

The thing that keeps coming through time and time again from people who have recovered is that you should assume absolutely nothing about your host site. It is very very easy to make assumptions that your kinds of standards and practice (in terms of software, particularly) will apply on the host site. Software and standards will undoubtedly differ from what you have. Even basic utilities may be different versions from the ones you have, because the other site is at a different stage. They may not be as up to date as you are, or they might be in advance of your own site. Lack of simple utilities in the right versions kills many application suites at the first attempt to run them.

Consider also the need for off-site security storage. Off-site storage is vital for four things: programs and data, documentation, stationery and spare media, and the contingency plan itself.

You need your data and your program libraries obviously, but your own may be totally inaccessible on your home site. You may not be able to get at them even though they are not damaged. You need a complete set of current data and programs on some off-site storage. It can be many days before you can get at your own even if they are in fire-proof safes or vaults. In the Belfast Co-op case it was one week before the salvage people got down to the fire-proof safe. In the fire which struck Denis Ferranti at Bangor on a Wednesday it was Saturday morning before they recovered the safe. So, the fire-proof safe may not be available for many days after a fire. If you do not have access to other data you will be stuck.

You also need documentation. As well as operational documentation on how to run the suites, you need control documentation available off-site. It is not usually very easy to run an application if you have no information about current file generation numbers, what the current control figures should be, and so on. If the control documentation is not available to start from some reasonable point at the other location, then probably you cannot run the application sensibly.

You need very good operational documentation off-site, because you have to bear in mind that your own staff may not be available to run those applications on the other site. It is not a pleasant thought, but if you are planning, you have to consider that staff may be injured or even killed in a disaster. The people who know how to run the suites may not be the ones who are running them in stand-by. If your documentation is not of the kind that a competent operator can pick up and use, you may not be able to run the thing at all.

It is a striking fact that many disasters that we know about do occur out of hours. This is very fortunate. The boiler explosion at Bowaters happened on a Sunday. The boiler went up through the computer room and up through the data preparation area leaving holes five metres wide in the floors. In normal times there were more than twenty data preparation clerks working on the one floor. Fortunately, at the time of the disaster there were only two people on site. If the explosion had happened in normal working hours, almost all the people would have been at least in hospital, if not dead.

In a flood which affected one site at Bristol they lost half their documentation. The documents were actually in the flood water and were unrecognisable and unusable. They said that although they lost 50% of the documents, it felt like 100% and it took them about 4 years to recover that documentation. You need storage for that kind of documentation in duplicate away from your site.

Think about special stationery. The lead time to print special stationery, like invoices, tends to be 3 or 4 weeks. If you do not have stationery available then you cannot sensibly do invoicing runs, for instance. Listing paper is less of a problem. It may not be quite the right size, but at least you can get things out.

Finally, but often overlooked, is that the disaster plan itself must be available off-site.

In connection with off-site storage you need regular schedules for moving stuff, updating media, documentation, and so on to and from the off-site stores. You need to audit that movement to make sure it does occur. It is very easy to assume that all is in order. Because the van arrives and people shift some stuff down and bring other stuff back, you assume that what exists out there is what you think it ought to be. If nobody really checks, this may not be so. Someone should audit the records against what is held in the off-site stores. They should check that the arrangements do work, and continue to work. Otherwise you may well find the deficiencies only when disaster strikes.

Mutual back-up arrangements for off-site storage could help if people were only aware of the advantages. If you can find some-body trustworthy on the other side of the town, who also has an installation, it may be quite easy to arrange facilities. All that is needed is a lockable storeroom at either end with access at all times, and transport across the town. That is quite an easy way of securing off-site storage, but people tend to be very reluctant to come to such arrangements. Banks and security companies provide facilities commercially.

All the evidence shows that you should schedule tests of stand-by regularly on your priority-one applications. You should concentrate effort on the ones that are important. Check-out that the application really works on the other site, and that capacity is still available. Remember the growth problem in normal times. If you take an assessment in July, it may be that by the end of that year your application has grown so much that the back-up site is no longer big enough to handle it. One of the retail chains reported that they had got back-up for a very large machine on four other machines, splitting the applications. They did a sizing exercise, and found everything to be satisfactory, even carrying out tests. However, within nine months the business had grown to such an extent that the back-up capacity available was no longer enough to run their applications. Consider the loadings at peak times, as well as the average loading. Very often you find that something grows during the year. It is quite small at the beginning of the year but it gets bigger and bigger towards the year end. The length of runs increases. It may be that you have adequate capacity to run at the beginning of the year, but not enough at the back end. A long job on a big machine can become an infinite job on a medium sized machine, so do a sizing exercise to make sure that your back-up is big enough and can cope.

11 Insurance

GENERAL

Insurance is one of the most common ways of transferring risks, or their consequences, from one party to another. The other common way of doing this is by contract – as in a maintenance contract for hardware, where the manufacturer agrees to keep the machine in working order, and to repair or replace any defective parts.

Insurance is a vital part of a risk management programme. Some risks can result in losses that are too big for the organisation to absorb. Destruction of a main plant by fire is a typical example. The actual loss, should it occur, is very big. Fortunately the frequency of such fires is very low. The average annual loss will be quite small for any enterprise, though the actual loss in a real event may be quite unacceptable. Insurance provides a mechanism for sharing the losses among many enterprises. It is a way of transferring the risk.

Transfer of risk by insurance is a passive technique, seeking to regain rather than to prevent loss. The risks are transferred to an insurance company by means of an insurance policy. The insurance company charges a premium for providing the cover for the risks, or their consequences. The policy then provides monetary compensation to the insured if the risk should occur. Insurance does not alter the risk, but it does affect the consequences.

The premiums charged will reflect the insurance companys' estimates of the risks. The premiums must be sufficiently big to cover the liabilities, else the insurance company will not be able to meet its obligations.

Computer insurance is still a comparatively new field. The traditional separation of insurance into different departments dealing with different classes of risk (fire, accident, life) made it difficult for companies to respond. The very complexity of computer systems, and the integration of the systems into business, increased the difficulties.

A general-purpose computer package policy may be satisfactory, but there are dangers. Computer insurance is best considered with the other insurances of a business. If the two are handled separately there is likely to be some overlap. The general insurance and the computer insurance may both cover the same risks, increasing the cost but not the real cover. More important though, is that there may be gaps. The cover provided by the two insurances may not, so to speak, meet up. If the computer insurance is considered as part of the general insurances carried by the business these difficulties can be avoided.

Special computer insurance tends to concentrate attention on the computer itself. The risk management approach demands that one looks at the whole enterprise, not just one part. One should take a comprehensive view of the risks that threaten the organisation. The policies should cover the risks for which insurance cover has been selected, without gaps and if possible without duplication.

Insurance is commonly used to cover three broad categories of loss. These are:

— material damage;

— business interruption;

— risks to and from personnel.

Material damage is the most obvious kind of insurance. It is used to cover the losses that arise directly from external events and internal breakdown. An all risks policy covers the insured for damage for all risks except those that are specifically excluded. It gives cover against accidental damage for risks such as: fire, explosion, theft, water, storm damage, malfunction of other equipment, vandalism and possibly malicious damage. The policy could perhaps best be described as 'almost all risks'. Cheaper cover can be had by excluding some risks: this is called 'selected perils'.

It is possible to obtain insurance for breakdown, which can supplement the benefits obtainable under maintenance contracts.

The fundamental principle of insurance is indemnity, which can best be described as exact financial compensation. An indemnity policy restores the insured to the same financial position after a loss as he enjoyed prior to the loss. It does not allow him to make a profit from his loss. Usually therefore any depreciation and loss of value by wear and tear will be taken into account. There is therefore no point in insuring an asset for more than its current value. If the sum insured (which is the maximum liability of the insured) is less than the current value then full indemnity is not available. The effect of this is that the insured is still carrying some of the risk.

It is sometimes possible to obtain cover on a 'replacement as new' basis. This 'new for old' concession modifies the indemnity principle. It is usually much more expensive, since the sum at risk is the full new replacement cost of the asset.

The principle of average is very important, and penalises those who under-insure. Where the sum insured is less than the value of the item that is being insured, an average clause means that the insured is paid less than he would have been. If the insurance is for 50% of the value of the item, then the insured will receive only 50% of any loss sustained.

In the event of total loss the insured is automatically penalised by the inadequacy of the sum insured. The insured is also penalised in a partial loss situation. This may not become apparent until too late, when the loss is sustained. The moral is to keep insured value in line with current value. Both under- and over-insurance should be avoided. The former leaves losses unprotected: the latter wastes money.

The other common feature is an excess clause, designed to avoid a number of small claims. The insurer pays only that part of a claim for damage which is in excess of some fixed amount. The damage up to this amount is the responsibility of the insured. Excess clauses are very common. They mean that the insured retains quite a significant portion of the risk – all the small claims, in fact. The insured may in practice be retaining quite a proportion of the annual loss exposure in this way.

Instead of an excess, the policy may have a franchise. In this case the insurer pays the whole claim if it is over the amount of the franchise. Again, damage which is less than the amount of the franchise is the responsibility of the insured. The effect on retention of risk is very similar.

BUSINESS INTERRUPTION

If the computer installation suffers damage the computer system may not be able to function normally. The business will be interrupted to a greater or lesser extent, and financial losses will follow.

These will include loss of revenue and loss of profit, because of the inability to produce goods or services. There will also be increased cost of working, due to costs on another machine, extra staff, overtime pay, transport and accommodation. Material damage is not the only reason for business interruption. It may, for instance, be incurred because of denial of access or loss of power supplies. Business interruption insurance can provide cover for these financial losses. This class of insurance is also called 'Consequential Loss Insurance' and 'Loss of Profits Insurance'. There is no obligation to take out consequential loss insurance for all the risks that are covered in a material damage policy, but the two are usually linked. The period of cover and the total sum insured for business interruption losses must be based on realistic estimates of the losses and costs that might be encountered. All experience is that costs far exceed initial estimates.

Cover is provided for a fixed period, called the indemnity period. Losses and costs continue for a long time after the event. The indemnity period is not unlimited, but is defined in the policy. During the indemnity period the insurer is liable for the specified costs and losses. Thereafter these fall to the insured. The usual 12 months is often inadequate, and two years may be much more sensible. It is quite hard to have too much cover for business interruption losses. It is cheap beforehand. Too little cover is often crippling, causing business failure.

Care should be taken not to confuse the indemnity period with the renewal period of the policy. For example, a policy might have a renewal date of 1 January. An insured event in December with a

12-month indemnity period would provide for losses and costs almost through the next calendar year.

Risks arising from personnel are quite varied. Injuries to persons must be covered by Employer's Liability and Public Liability Insurance. Absence of employees can be covered by a Health and Sickness Policy. Dishonest acts can be covered by a Fidelity Guarantee Policy. Risks from personnel negligence can be covered, as can those arising from breach of duty. Special care ought to be given to personnel risks in a stand-by mode of working. Are employees covered if they are working elsewhere? What about damage they might cause to the equipment and facilities at the host site. It may be covered in a contract between the two organisations, but there may be no contract if the arrangement was concluded hurriedly between the two DPMs.

The final point to bear in mind about insurance, of whatever kind, is the principle of 'utmost good faith'. Each party to the contract of insurance is under a duty to disclose all material facts to the other. A material fact is one that could have a bearing on the assessment of the risk situation. For example, if the site contains a store of combustible material, this is likely to be pertinent to any assessment of the fire risk.

If material facts are withheld the policy may be declared invalid when the facts come to light. The insured is not penalised for not revealing facts that he did not know, and could not reasonably be expected to know. Usually the policy contains conditions that require the insured to notify the insurer of any changes that could have a bearing on the risk. In case of doubt it is best to consult anyway.

12 Data Protection and Privacy

The debate about computers and personal information began in the United States in the late 1960s, and was taken up shortly afterwards in this country. There was growing concern about the way computer systems might be used to handle personal information. The increasing size and complexity of computer-based systems raised fears about possible abuses. Citizens became concerned about the possible misuse of personal information by government and some commercial organisations. George Orwell's *1984* did not seem too far away.

Several attempts have been made to formulate a satisfactory definition of privacy. 'Privacy is the claim of individuals, groups or institutions to determine for themselves when, how and to what extent information about them is communicated to others' (Westin). Another definition is 'the individual's ability to control the circulation of information relating to him' (Miller). These definitions suggest that possession of data does not carry with it absolute rights to decide how and when that data shall be processed. Privacy carries with it the idea that the user of data must in some way respect the legitimate wishes of the data subject.

There are three parties with an interest in personal information in a computer system. First is the data user, who controls the storage and processing of the data. Until recently the data user has assumed that he can process the data in any way he chooses. The data subject is the second party with an interest in the data. The data subject is one of the individuals about whom the data user holds information. There is also a third interest, that of the rest of society, of the public at large. There will sometimes be some conflict of interest between these three parties about what data should be handled.

Privacy is an Anglo-Saxon concept, not well understood in continental Europe. There attention has focussed rather on the idea of data protection. Data protection is concerned with the ethical use of data. It may involve restrictions on the kind of data that is held in computer systems and the way in which it is used.

Data protection might mean that inaccurate data should not be used, or that certain classes of data cannot be collected and stored.

Privacy and data protection overlap, but they are not synonymous, though they do have much in common. They are concerned particularly with the handling of sensitive information about people. The first problem is to decide what kinds of information are sensitive. This is by no means as simple as it might seem.

Medical information is usually regarded as especially sensitive, and details about a person's medical history are treated with discretion. Care is taken about their confidentiality. With other sorts of information – eg race, religion, nationality and even name and address details – the sensitivity varies with time and place.

Different societies see different kinds of personal information in various ways. Some people are willing to allow more information about themselves to be known than others. Differences of age, views, beliefs, temperament and personality all have a part to play. It is often surprising how much information someone will reveal if they see an advantage in doing so. It may be the prospect of a financial gain, or the desire to be elected to some office, that provides the motive.

There is a surprising lack of agreement about what is sensitive. In the UK and especially in England the use of name and address files for mail-shots is portrayed as an invasion of privacy. The passing-on and use of mailing lists are depicted in the media as somehow ethically wrong. The idea is that a person's residential address is not a matter of public property. This extends even to business addresses in some cases. There have been complaints about the sale and use of addresses derived from the Yellow Pages business telephone directories.

This is a very strange idea in Sweden and Germany. In Sweden the government maintains a public register of the name and address of all citizens. The compilation of this list is a parliamentary monopoly. It is readily available to all who need it. In Germany everyone's address is on a government register. When people move house they must notify the authorities. In consequence citizens in such cultures do not regard their address as very private.

All citizens in Sweden have a national number. The first part of the number is the date of birth. People are quite open about their number, and therefore age and date of birth are not so sensitive as they are in Britain.

In contrast, nationality is a sensitive matter in Sweden. This may have origins in the traditional neutrality of the country. The Data Inspection Board does not allow storage of nationality in computer systems as a rule. On a typical personnel administration and payroll system nationality is coded in three categories. These are Swedish, Scandinavian and other. The second group is needed because of the common employment market in the Scandinavian countries.

Data protection and privacy are now very complex. Many countries have introduced laws to regulate the use of personal information. Sometimes these laws govern all the use of personal information. In most cases the regulations apply only when some automatic means of processing (eg a computer) is used. The law sometimes applies to government systems only, or there may be differences between its application in the public and private sectors.

The other major distinction is the question of legal persons. The legislation in Austria, Belgium, Luxembourg and Norway applies to natural persons and legal persons. In other words companies and other legal entities are protected as well as ordinary individuals. This greatly extends the scope of any regulations. Almost any business records about relations with others would be covered. Sales, purchases and marketing are affected, as well as payroll and personnel records. There has been considerable debate about the wisdom of introducing such protection. For one thing it introduces problems of definition, especially in an international trading context.

There are two important international agreements in this area. These are the OECD Guidelines and the European Convention.

The OECD *Guidelines Governing the Protection of Privacy and Transborder Flows of Personal Data* have been adopted internationally. They define eight principles about personal data and its use. These are:

PART TWO – BASIC PRINCIPLES OF NATIONAL APPLICATION

Collection limitation principle

7 There should be limits to the collection of personal data and any such data should be obtained by lawful and fair means and, where appropriate, with the knowledge or consent of the data subject.

Data quality principle

8 Personal data should be relevant to the purposes for which they are to be used, and, to the extent necessary for those purposes, should be accurate, complete and kept up-to-date.

Purpose specification principle

9 The purposes for which personal data are collected should be specified not later than at the time of data collection and the subsequent use limited to the fulfilment of those purposes or such others as are not incompatible with those purposes and as are specified on each occasion of change of purpose.

Use limitation principle

10 Personal data should not be disclosed, made available or otherwise used for purposes other than those specified in accordance with Paragraph 9 except:

a) with the consent of the data subject; or

b) by the authority of law.

Security safeguards principle

11   Personal data should be protected by reasonable security safeguards against such risks as loss or unauthorized access, destruction, use, modification or disclosure of data.

Openness principle

12   There should be a general policy of openness about developments, practices and policies with respect to personal data. Means should be readily available of establishing the existence and nature of personal data, and the main purposes of their use, as well as the identity and usual residence of the data controller.

Individual participation principle

13   An individual should have the right:

a)   to obtain from a data controller, or otherwise, confirmation of whether or not the data controller has data relating to him;

b)   to have communicated to him, data relating to him

    i)   within a reasonable time;

    ii)   at a charge, if any, that is not excessive;

    iii) in a reasonable manner; and

    iv)   in a form that is readily intelligible to him;

c)   to be given reasons if a request made under sub-paragraphs (a) and (b) is denied, and to be able to challenge such denial; and

d)   to challenge data relating to him and, if the challenge is successful, to have the data erased, rectified, completed or amended.

Accountability principle

14   A data controller should be accountable for complying with measures which give effect to the principles stated above.

   The other major international initiative is the Council of Europe *Convention for the Protection of Individuals with Regard to Automatic Processing of Personal Data.* This also has eight principles for data protection:

CHAPTER II – BASIC PRINCIPLES FOR DATA PROTECTION

Article 4 – Duties of the Parties

1   Each Party shall take the necessary measures in its domestic law to give effect to the basic principles for data protection set out in this chapter.

2   These measures shall be taken at the latest at the time of entry into force of this Convention in respect of that Party.

Article 5 – Quality of data

Personal data undergoing automatic processing shall be:

a) obtained and processed fairly and lawfully;

b) stored for specified and legitimate purposes and not used in a way incompatible with those purposes;

c) adequate, relevant and not excessive in relation to the purposes for which they are stored;

d) accurate and, where necessary, kept up-to-date;

e) preserved in a form which permits identification of the data subjects for no longer than is required for the purpose for which those data are stored.

Article 6 – Special categories of data

Personal data revealing racial origin, political opinions or religious or other beliefs, as well as personal data concerning health or sexual life, may not be processed automatically unless domestic law provides appropriate safeguards. The same shall apply to personal data relating to criminal convictions.

Article 7 – Data security

Appropriate security measures shall be taken for the protection of personal data stored in automated data files against accidental or unauthorized destruction or accidental loss as well as against unauthorized access, alteration or dissemination.

Article 8 – Additional safeguards for the data subject

Any person shall be enabled:

a) to establish the existence of an automated personal data file, its main purpose, as well as the identity and habitual residence or principal place of business of the controller of the file;

b) to obtain at reasonable intervals and without excessive delay or expense confirmation of whether personal data relating to him are stored in the automated data file as well as communication to him of such data in an intelligible form;

c) to obtain, as the case may be, rectification or erasure of such data if these have been processed contrary to the provisions of domestic law giving effect to the basic principles set out in Articles 5 and 6 of this Convention;

d) to have a remedy if a request for confirmation or, as the case may be, communication, rectification or erasure as referred to in paragraphs (b) and (c) of this article is not complied with.

Article 9 – Exceptions and restrictions

1 No exception to the provisions of Articles 5, 6 and 8 of this Convention shall be allowed except within the limits defined in this article.

2 Derogation from the provisions of Articles 5, 6 and 8 of this Convention shall be allowed when such derogation is provided for by law of the Party and constitutes a necessary measure in a democratic society in the interests of:

a) protecting State security, public safety, the monetary interests of the State or the suppression of criminal offences;

b) protecting the data subject or the rights and freedoms of others.

3 Restrictions on the exercise of the rights specified in Article 8, paragraphs (b), (c) and (d) may be provided by law with respect to automatic personal data files used for statistics or for scientific research purposes when there is obviously no risk of an infringement of the privacy of the data subjects.

Article 10 – Sanctions and remedies

Each Party undertakes to establish appropriate sanctions and remedies for violations of provisions of domestic law giving effect to the basic principles for data protection set out in this chapter.

Article 11 – Extended protection

None of the provisions of this chapter shall be interpreted as limiting or otherwise affecting the possibility for a Party to grant data subjects a wider measure of protection than that stipulated in this Convention.

It is significant that both agreements demand appropriate security safeguards to protect the information from unauthorised disclosure. Most security measures are designed to guard against loss or damage. Loss of confidentiality is often much harder to protect. If a physical thing is stolen you can see that it is missing. If information is disclosed there may be no evidence that this has happened.

The accountability principle of the OECD convention also means that the auditability is important. Data protection/privacy regulations impose certain duties on the data user. The data user must be able to demonstrate that he took reasonable steps to protect the data, and to control access. These things must be auditable.

In some countries the authorities have the power to inspect installations for compliance with the established regulations. Such external inspection need not be expensive. Financial systems have been subject to external audit for many years. The auditor examines the system, on behalf of the shareholders. If he is satisfied he issues a certificate that the accounts give a true and fair view. He gives no absolute guarantee, of course. In a practical world the auditor cannot examine every transaction. Equally there can be no absolute assurance that there will never be breaches of data protection, even in well conducted enterprises.

It is reassuring that there have been relatively very few breaches reported in the media over the years. This indicates that most organisations take a good deal of care with personal data. One life assurance company pointed out that they had been in business for over 100 years and had lost no information in that time. Standards generally are very high in the UK in this area.

Any commercial organisation with adequate controls and security on its financial systems should have little trouble with data protection regulation. It may need to make changes to meet the proposed regulations. Those organisations with poor controls and lax auditors may have problems. The biggest difficulty in introducing data protection regulation is a cultural one. So long as data users ignore the legitimate aspirations of data subjects there will be problems.

This is illustrated by a comment from the Data Processing Manager of a major UK company. 'The regulations would only apply to government systems, of course, not to payroll and things like that?'

Regulation of information processing activities is a fact of life in much of Europe. Further laws will come, on topics like transborder data flows, freedom of information and so on. It may take a generation to come to terms with the shift in attitude. Security for information systems is an essential part of the process.

Further Reading

This short list of computer security books and collections is not exhaustive. New works appear all the time. Comprehensive annotated bibliographies are given by Brown and Ellison in particular. These contain references to several hundred papers and articles.

Specialist periodicals include:

International Security Review, quarterly, UNISAF Publications Ltd

Security Gazette, monthly, Security Gazette Ltd

Both these cover the whole security field, but features on access control, fire, and so on are relevant to any security programme.

Computer Security Journal, Computer Security Institute

The two 1981 issues contain a good range of professional computer security papers.

Computer Fraud and Security Bulletin, Elsevier International Bulletins

Started by M J Comer – see below – this contains many accounts of actual breaches of computer security, with analysis of the causes and possible defences. Not too technical, and often entertaining reading.

EDPACS The EDP Audit Control and Security Newsletter, Automation Training Centre Inc, Reston, Virginia 22090

A 'must' for any serious student of computer systems security. EDPACS is transatlantic in outlook, but always contains many interesting and useful items.

Computers and Security, North Holland Publishing Company

Devoted to the technical and financial aspects of computer security, the first number was published in January 1982. It is a specialist journal.

Other computer and accountancy periodicals frequently include relevant material. The early literature had no other home.

Useful books and collections include:

BloomBecker J, Who Are The Computer Criminals?, *New Scientist,* 13 March 1980, Vol 85, No 1198

A popular account of some of the classes of deliberate attack on computer systems.

Broadbent D, *Contingency Planning,* NCC Publications (1979)

Describes how to assess the dependence of an organisation on computers, what might put them out of action, and how to prepare a contingency plan.

Brown P S (ed), *Computer Security Manual,* Computer Security Institute, Hudson, Massachusetts (1981)

This edited compilation of about forty reprints of key papers and articles is issued annually to members of the institute. Mainly US origin it is a convenient and useful way of building a library. The newsletter is also very practical in outlook.

Carroll J M, *Computer Security,* Security World Publishing Co (1977)

This book discusses the management and organisation of security, physical security, threat evaluation and personnel aspects.

CIPFA, *Guidance on Fraud Investigation,* Chartered Institute of Public Finance and Accountancy (1980)

A short explanation of what to do, and not to do, if faced with the possibility of fraud. It includes recommended practice and an explanation of the legal factors. Highly recommended.

Comer M J, *Corporate Fraud,* McGraw Hill (1977)

The standard work on all aspects of corporate fraud. It contains much relevant material.

Computer Fraud Survey, Local Government Audit Inspectorate, 1981

The results of a survey including 67 cases, with full details in many instances.

Ellison J R, *Computer Systems Security,* Pergamon Infotech (1981)

This comprehensive state of the art report includes 16 invited papers, as well as a detailed editorial analysis over 150 pages long.

Fire Protection for Electronic Data Processing Installations (British Standard Code of Practice). BS 6266: 1982 British Standards Institution

This is a revision of the earlier code CP95. It is written for the specialist.

Goldblum E, *Computer Disasters and Contingency Planning,* Amdahl/Butler Cox (1982)

Intended for senior management, this report covers threats to computer installations, how companies actually did plan for disaster, and gives a guide for planning.

Lindop Sir Norman, *Report of the Committee on Data Protection,* HMSO 1978

One of the most detailed analyses of data protection ever produced. Still a most useful work, even though it was not acted upon by the government.

Martin J, *Security, Accuracy and Privacy in Computer Systems,* Prentice Hall (1973)

Now becoming somewhat dated, this is still useful as background material.

National Bureau of Standards, *Guideline for Automatic Data Processing Risk Analysis,* US Department of Commerce FIPS PUB 65 (1979)

Chapters include: the role of management, preliminary security examination, risk analysis and selection of safeguards. Based on the techniques developed by Courtney for IBM, it contains a great deal of practical good sense.

National Fire Prevention and Control Administration, *Standard Practice for the Fire Protection of Essential Electronic Equipment,* US Department of Commerce RP-1 (1978)

Despite its formidable title this is a most practical guide to fire protection thinking. Contains many details of actual fires as cautioning tales. It should be treated with caution by readers outside the States since different rules apply elsewhere.

Parker D B, *Crime by Computer,* Charles Scribner's & Sons, New York (1976)

Based on practical investigation of several hundred cases of computer crime, this is a very readable treatment by a world authority.

Pritchard J A T, *Data Encryption,* NCC Publications (1980)

Provides a full explanation of data encryption and information about how organisations might use it.

Pritchard J A T, *Risk Management in Action,* NCC Publications (1978)

Contains detailed information about practical application of various kinds of risk analysis and control techniques.

Pritchard J A T, *Security in On-line Systems,* NCC Publications (1979)

Covers all aspects of communications and on-line systems security using traditional circuit switching techniques.

Recommendations for the Protection of Computer Installations Against Fire, Fire Offices' Committee (1979)

This gives detailed recommendations for construction equipment and space protection including floor and ceiling voids. Air conditioning and protection of records are covered. There are specifications for halon and carbon dioxide flooding systems.

SECURITECH, *The International Guide to Security Equipment,* UNISAF Publications

This is an annual catalogue of all kinds of physical security products. Fully illustrated and in four languages, it gives a wealth of detail.

Simons G L, *Privacy in The Computer Age,* NCC Publications (1982)

Profiles the areas of concern, and details the factors that have led up to the present UK government plans for legislation.

Squires T, *Computer Security— The Personnel Aspect,* NCC Publications (1980)

This covers protection from people and protection of people in computer systems. Personnel and training aspects, and the effects of health and safety legislation are covered, as well as people in contingency situations.

Thomas A J and Douglas I J, *Audit of Computer Systems,* NCC Publications (1981)

Examines the role and requirements of the auditor in relation to system development, routine and statutory audit.

Waring L P, *Management Handbook of Computer Security,* NCC Publications (1978)

A very detailed guide to computer security using the risk management approach. Many checklists are included, making it an invaluable tool for any practitioner.

Waring L P, *Planning for Standby*, NCC Publications (1976)

Provides practical guidance and checklists of the many factors that should be considered in planning for disaster back-up.

Wong K K, *Risk Analysis and Control*, NCC Publications (1977)

Develops a detailed method for analysing risks to corporate computer systems, including the many facets outside DP. It includes explanations of several methodologies.

Index

127